MW01100628

EDIZIONI

ARCHITECTURE in the PUBLIC INTEREST
FENTRESS BRADBURN ARCHITECTS

EDIZIONI PRESS

COPYRIGHT (C) 2001 *by* EDIZIONI PRESS, INC.

All rights reserved. No part of this book may be reproduced in any form
without written permission of the copyright owners.
All images in this book have been reproduced with the consent of the artists
concerned and no responsibility is accepted by producer,
publisher or printer for any infringement of copyright or otherwise, arising
from the contents of this publication. Every effort has been
made to ensure that credits comply with information supplied.

FIRST PUBLISHED IN
THE UNITED STATES OF AMERICA

by EDIZIONI PRESS, INC.
469 WEST 21ST STREET
NEW YORK, NEW YORK 10011
MAIL@EDIZIONIPRESS.COM

ISBN: 1-931536-00-7
LIBRARY OF CONGRESS CATALOGUE
CARD NUMBER: 2001086704
PRINTED *in* ITALY

DESIGN AND COMPOSITION: Ethan Trask
EDITORIAL DIRECTOR: Anthony Iannacci
ASSISTANT EDITOR: Jamie Schwartz
EDITORIAL ASSISTANTS: Kara Janeczko, Aaron Seward
SPECIAL THANKS TO: Tymmie Serr, Betsy Connors, Jessica Sommers
and Val Moses of Fentress Bradburn Architects Ltd.
FRONT AND BACK COVER: "City of Oakland Administration Buildings;
Oakland, California" Photographs by Nick Merrick, Hedrich Blessing

■ INTRODUCTION

7   ACKNOWLEDGEMENTS
JIM BRADBURN, FAIA

8-11   TOWARD A CRITICAL REGIONALISM
DAVID DILLON

12-15   DESIGNING PUBLIC SPACE: PROCESSES/CONCEPTS/IDEAS
CURT FENTRESS, FAIA

■ CIVIC BUILDINGS

18-25   CITY OF OAKLAND ADMINISTRATION BUILDINGS *OAKLAND, CALIFORNIA*

26-33   DAVID E. SKAGGS FEDERAL BUILDING, *BOULDER, COLORADO*

34-41   CLARK COUNTY GOVERNMENT CENTER *CLARK COUNTY, NEVADA*

42-45   REGIONAL TRANSPORTATION COMMISSION and
REGIONAL FLOOD CONTROL DISTRICT HEADQUARTERS *CLARK COUNTY, NEVADA*

46-51   JEFFERSON COUNTY COURTS AND ADMINISTRATION BUILDING *GOLDEN, COLORADO*

52-55   LARIMER COUNTY JUSTICE CENTER *FORT COLLINS, COLORADO*

56-57   CIVIC CENTER PARKING STRUCTURE *FORT COLLINS, COLORADO*

■ AIRPORTS

60-67   SEOUL INCHON INTERNATIONAL AIRPORT PASSENGER TERMINAL
INCHON, KOREA

68-71   SEATTLE-TACOMA INTERNATIONAL AIRPORT CENTRAL TERMINAL REDEVELOPMENT
SEATTLE, WASHINGTON

72-83   DENVER INTERNATIONAL AIRPORT PASSENGER TERMINAL COMPLEX
DENVER, COLORADO

84-89   DOHA INTERNATIONAL AIRPORT
DOHA, QATAR

90-95   VIENNA INTERNATIONAL AIRPORT TERMINAL COMPLEX EXPANSION, DESIGN COMPETITION
VIENNA, AUSTRIA

■ MUSEUMS + THEATERS

98-103   NATIONAL MUSEUM OF WILDLIFE ART *JACKSON, WYOMING*

104-107   BUFFALO BILL HISTORICAL CENTER *CODY, WYOMING*

108-115   NATIONAL COWBOY HALL OF FAME *OKLAHOMA CITY, OKLAHOMA*

116-121   PEERY'S EGYPTIAN THEATER
and THE DAVID ECCLES CONFERENCE CENTER *OGDEN, UTAH*

■ RECENT WORK

124-129   DENVER BRONCOS STADIUM *DENVER, COLORADO*

130-133   KUWAIT FINANCE HOUSE TOWER *KUWAIT CITY, KUWAIT*

134-137   421 BROADWAY *DENVER, COLORADO*

138-141   COLORADO CHRISTIAN UNIVERSITY *LAKEWOOD, COLORADO*

■ APPENDIX

142-143   CREDITS

THE VARIOUS FUNCTIONS
AT JEFFERSON COUNTY COURTS
AND ADMINISTRATION BUILDING
(GOLDEN, COLORADO)
ARE SEPARATED INTO TWO ARCS THAT
ARE JOINED BY A CENTRAL ROTUNDA.

tance of what takes place within. "It is important to go beyond the walls and create a setting for a building," says Fentress. "I.M Pei was brilliant at standing back and looking at the big picture in order to make a total environment. This might involve adding a few trees or changing the direction of an approach, but it made a huge difference. Using berms at Jefferson County and a long armature of trees in Las Vegas are my way of doing the same thing."

Fentress Bradburn got the Larimer County and Clark County commissions through competitions, which have buttressed the practice from the beginning. Competitions are risky ventures, the architectural equivalent of roulette, in which enormous amounts of capital and emotional energy are bet on a single roll of the dice. On the other hand, winning a major competition can propel a firm from obscurity to celebrity almost overnight.

Fentress Bradburn parlayed their initial success in the Colorado Convention Center competition into the commission for the Denver International Airport, which in turn generated other airport commissions around the world. Competitions are collaborative efforts that bring the firm together, and generate invaluable creative capital that, even in a loss, can be deposited in an intellectual savings account for future use.

"They're essential for sharpening your design skills," says Fentress. "There's nothing like a competition to get the juices going and remind you of why you became an architect."

THE NEW ATRIUM, AT CENTER,
AT THE NATIONAL COWBOY HALL
OF FAME (OKLAHOMA CITY,
OKLAHOMA) BLENDS WITH THE
EXISTING FACILITY.

A graduate of I.M Pei's office and one of the first employees of Kohn Pedersen Fox, Curt Fentress learned how to grow a firm from experts. At Pei, he discovered the importance of collaboration and the value of such apparent luxuries as a model shop, which Fentress Bradburn has. At Kohn Pedersen Fox, he learned how to think like a client, how to use the office as a sales tool — the model gallery in the lobby of Fentress Bradburn's office was inspired by a similar space at KPF — and how to take chances.

In Denver, Curt is the principal who directs design while Jim oversees production. Bradburn describes the division of labor like this: "Curt is the principal in charge of promises and I'm the principal in charge of delivery." But the line between design and production is not nearly as rigid as it was at Roche Dinkeloo. The architects work in project teams instead of studios. Each team functions as a sort of office, to which the principals serve as critics and advisors. Bradburn meets regularly with each team to assess the status of projects, including whether or not it is making money. "It's fascinating to me to know where every project is every day, financially as well as architecturally. I got that from John Dinkeloo." The firm has also completed ten design-build projects, starting with the Colorado Convention Center, which have expanded the range and versatility of the practice.

Fentress Bradburn expects to grow to 150 employees within the next few years. Although the firm continues to expand, it refuses to grow fat and complacent. The work that is coming out of the firm these days is as diverse and ambitious as that of many large coastal firms. Courthouses, office buildings and convention centers continue to be a major part of the mix. (The firm recently won the commission for a $270 million expansion of the Colorado Convention Center.) And the firm continues to be one of the leading airport designers in the world, with recent designs for projects in Seattle/Tacoma, Vienna, Madrid and Tenerife-Sur. Their new stadium for the Denver Broncos football team is a sculptural contemporary design that bucks the current retro craze in sports architecture. Design is underway for an $80 million air museum in Kalamazoo, Michigan, along with several office buildings, the conversion of a former rubber factory into an e-commerce incubator and a number of major planning studies.

Instead of finding a comfortable niche and settling in, Fentress Bradburn continues to reinvent itself, expanding into new areas and rethinking its place in familiar ones.

"It still feels like a big experiment," insists Bradburn. "There's a youthful questioning quality to much of what we do, and I hope that continues."

THE BOWL OF THE BRONCO
STADIUM (DENVER, COLORADO)
BEGINS TO TAKE SHAPE AS
THE AUGUST 2001 OPENING
DATE APPROACHES.

AN EARLY DESIGN CONCEPT
FOR THE SEATTLE-TACOMA
INTERNATIONAL AIRPORT
(SEATTLE, WASHINGTON).

DESIGNING PUBLIC SPACE
PROCESSES/CONCEPTS/IDEAS

CURT FENTRESS, FAIA

A passion for designing to region and context has figured significantly in our work, but the true importance of this approach lies in the higher ideal it serves: humanism. Tying buildings to their region and context strengthens the human sense of structures and puts users at the center of the design.

The rigors of public architecture have been the crucible in which we have tested our ideas about humanizing architecture. Civic buildings tend to be larger, to have more users, to encompass a greater number of purposes. Designers must therefore give these buildings a comfortable scale and a clear plan. But the greatest design challenge is in symbolism, which in the best civic architecture manifests as a ceremonial quality that provides a felt connection with community.

A building's aesthetics and the emotional response it evokes should work on behalf of this human need to connect—for instance, by embodying the welcoming arms of open and accessible government. But, in addition to such universal forms and gestures, this need can be addressed through the use of native materials, references to context or the introduction of design elements that are evocative of region and culture. All of these aesthetic elements enrich the experience of a building, heightening users' awareness of the space and how it connects with the landscape and the collective civic spirit. Designed well, a public building reinforces and enhances the experience of community.

Our concern with both the humanistic and functional issues of design makes public work a natural choice for Fentress Bradburn Architects. However, even these natural affinities were only a beginning for us. Each project has taught us about the process of creating public structures and, over time, certain constants have emerged. These are less guideposts than they are touchstones—ideas that continue to surface each time our designs for public structures begin to take shape.

Our experience can be distilled into seven ideas: four design concepts that put the user foremost and three

humanistic ideas that have guided us from the first. I believe that in order to design successful public architecture, one must:

1) USE CONTEXT TO CREATE AN IDENTITY.
An architect can learn from a public building's context how to express its purpose. One may be inspired by landforms, use natural materials from the region or match the colors and textures of the environment. But one must keep foremost in mind the purpose of the building, the function it serves and its identity.

This can be done with soaring shapes for an airport, with more earth-bound forms to show solidity in government or in more subtle and playful ways. Let me give two examples from our work: We housed the Regional Flood Control District at Clark County, Nevada, within undulating "canyon" walls, which bring to mind the volatile resource that agency regulates. At the National Museum of Wildlife Art, we evoked the experience of discovery in wildlife observation by making the museum mysterious on first approach, blending it into the background as a natural stone outcropping.

2) LET CULTURE GUIDE DESIGN.
The culture—whether it's the culture of an entire country, that of a region or a corporate culture—can direct the architect. When designing airports in Qatar and Korea, we were led by cultural markers, including local sailing vessels, the lines of which helped us sustain the imagery of transit.

At the David E. Skaggs Federal Building, which houses the National Oceanic and Atmospheric Administration's research laboratories in Boulder, Colorado, we punctuated walls of locally quarried stone with atriums and stairwells constructed of sleek aluminum columns that bespeak the facility's scientific culture.

In the city of Oakland, California, we re-wove the city fabric by creating new administration buildings that were inspired and rooted in the traditions of the area's historic buildings, bringing new life to the area while still honoring the culture that already existed there.

3) CELEBRATE THE ENTRY.

To function well, a building must be easy to read from the outside, as well as from the inside. Users must know at a glance where to enter and, once inside, they should be directed with a minimum of graphics. At the same time, the architect should give users a moment of repose, to tell them they have arrived and to explain how the building works—a moment when, in a sense, the building greets the user.

The front door of the original National Cowboy Hall of Fame was very difficult to find. With our addition, we created a completely new entry that is prominent on the exterior. Inside, we placed the museum's largest sculpture on an axis with the entrance, emphasizing the atrium's hero-ic scale. This kind of detail helps to center the user within the building.

To create a sense of arrival in government facilities, we have used entries and rotundas, points from which the building radiates or branches out or encircles the user. We have made many of these glassy and bright, but some situations have called for other solutions. Las Vegas is surrounded by desert, where one seeks shade and rest from the light. For this reason, we made the central point of the Clark County Government Center a solid kiva-like form.

Inside Denver International Airport, users experience a sense of arrival upon entering the Great Hall, the openness

THE METAL RAIL DETAILS ON THE DAZIEL BUILDING (OAKLAND, CALIFORNIA) ARE A MODERN INTERPRETATION OF CLASSICAL CORNICE ORNAMENTATION, AS SEEN ON CITY HALL, AT RIGHT.

of which also helps people find their way. We placed taller skylighted masts at the two bridges that cross the cathedral-like interior of Denver International Airport to help organize the space for travelers.

4) DISCOVER THE NATURAL ORDER.

Many buildings with complex programs become mazes, simply by fulfilling all the needs called for to make them functional. The challenge for the architect of complex large-scale projects is to make it easy for users to find their way around. To do this, one must discover the natural order of the elements and organize them in a simple manner. In Jefferson, Larimer and Clark counties, we organized agencies based on the amount of public contact they have: The services used most often were made most accessible by putting those offices on the lowest floors.

5) STAY FOCUSED.

The public process tends to be long, protracted, bureaucratic, complex and vulnerable to political upheaval. Public buildings bring together many personalities and agendas, which make misunderstandings and conflicts much more likely. It is necessary for the architect to practice patience on all fronts and avoid getting swept up in the process itself, which can be halting in its progress and frustrating at times. The architect should remain open to all communication while cultivating an understanding that the public process is simply more intense than other design processes.

6) LISTEN CLOSELY.

For the architect, creating public architecture is not a tidy package or a simple task and it is seldom an easy process. The architect is answerable not just to one owner or a board of directors but to an entire community. At the same time, public architecture is one of the most exciting arenas in which an architect can work, balancing aesthetics and utilitarian concerns with program, public input and one's own inspiration.

Public input is a large part of the process of creating a civic building. There needs to be a relationship of trust and respect between the architect and the people who will work in the building, use the building, live near the building and pay for the building. We are often inspired by these people's thoughts, which usually reach our ears in public meetings, rather than in letters or reports or even notes.

This is an important point: These are people who literally want a voice in the design of the building. These people take the time to come to a meeting organized by the city or county or agency in question, and they find the courage to speak; to voice their passions, their desires and their frustrations; to take a stand; to offer their insight; and to invest their emotions. Part of the task of an architect of public buildings is to acknowledge these personal acts of community and to embody these voices.

At a cocktail party before the competition for the government center in Clark County, Nevada, I heard people say, "We're not all showgirls or gamblers or dealers." They wanted an alternative to The Strip; they wanted a place with dignity, where they could gather as a community of citizens. This is where the inspiration to add an amphitheater to the facility originated. If you go there to hear a classical music concert, you'll come away with a very different impression of those who live in Las Vegas than you would if you simply visited the casinos.

The public process can either kill a building or make great architecture. It can be a part of the creation of art, just as the potter's wheel is essential to the creation of pottery. But it is a tool one must learn how to use. The architect must understand the public process and respect it as a means to do more than just build a functional building. There's a certain flow to the process. You can see in many buildings of the '50s, '60s and '70s that the community and the architect suffered with this process. Without a good process, you don't get a good building.

7) RESTRAIN THE EGO.

A building's presence should speak. It should make a statement, but not a statement that overpowers the building's purpose, its operation, its landscape, its culture or the users who come to it. A building's statement should emerge from those very elements, and the architect should serve as their contact point. The moment of creativity for the architect should be neither a flight of fancy away from earthly or quotidian concerns nor a retreat into intellect and theory. Instead, the moment of creativity should be pure alchemy, a time when the user becomes central, when the place and the people and the program are allowed to speak through the architect, coming together to create a compelling structure.

FACING PAGE:
AN ABSTRACT IMAGE
OF AN OAK TREE, FOR
WHICH OAKLAND WAS
NAMED, GRACES THE
CEILING OF THE
DALZIEL BUILDING.

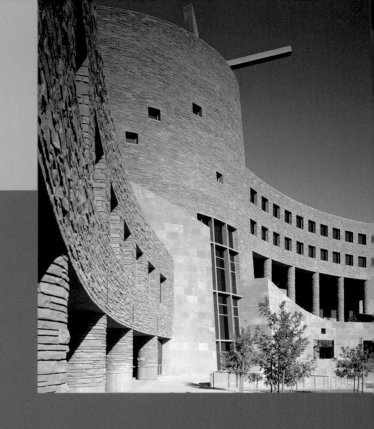

CIVIC BUILDINGS

*"Give users a moment of repose as they arrive—
a moment to meet the building and take it in.
If the architect has discovered the building's
natural order and designed to it, this moment
of repose can also orient the user to the building."*
- Curt Fentress

CITY OF OAKLAND
ADMINISTRATION BUILDINGS
OAKLAND, CALIFORNIA

When the city of Oakland, California, decided to rebuild its urban core after the devastating 1989 Loma Prieta earthquake, a prime concern was that the new civic center match the restored City Hall building aesthetically. The 1914 Beaux Arts-style City Hall had been structurally repaired and seismically retrofitted in 1997. In a national design competition held by the city to select the best team for the project, Fentress Bradburn was awarded first place, based on its ability to clearly understand how to represent civic architecture, establish user-friendly spaces and address both the history and future of Oakland.

The project's program consolidated 12 governmental agencies into one central location. Included in the project were The Dalziel Building, a new 354,000-square-foot office building, and the 190,000-square-foot renovation and expansion of the historic Broadway Building to create the new Lionel J. Wilson Building. The Wilson Building addition increased usable floor space, provided new systems and vertical circulation and gave seismic stability to this historic structure.

All aspects of the design respond to Oakland's historical architecture while evoking a new image for the city. To create this image, Fentress Bradburn focused on the stability and power of government, the beauty of Oakland's geography, the importance of democracy smoothly and efficiently serving the people and the essence of a growing city and its diverse population. The campus' pre-existing buildings were Renaissance in style, with tripartite exterior façades,

FACING PAGE:
THE CITY OF OAKLAND ADMINISTRATION BUILDINGS DO NOT OVERSHADOW THE BEAUX ARTS CITY HALL (LEFT), BUT TIE ALL THREE BUILDINGS TOGETHER IN A GRAND CIVIC SPACE. THE LIONEL J. WILSON BUILDING IS AT MIDDLE RIGHT; THE DALZIEL BUILDING IS AT UPPER LEFT.

LEFT:
MODEL ILLUSTRATES HOW THE THREE BUILDINGS ARE ORGANIZED WITHIN THE COMPLEX. PEDESTRIAN WALKWAYS AND THE FRANK H. OGAWA PLAZA SEPARATE THE BUILDINGS AND CREATE OUTDOOR GATHERING SPACES.

THIS PAGE
RIGHT:
THE OLD BROADWAY
BUILDING (AT RIGHT) IS
BLENDED WITH THE
NEW EXPANSION AND
ROTUNDA (AT LEFT) TO
CREATE THE WILSON
BUILDING.

BELOW:
THE WILSON BUILDING
ROTUNDA CREATES
A FOCAL POINT
FOR THE NEW FRANK
H. OGAWA PLAZA.

CENTER:
AN ORNAMENTAL
CROWN TOPS THE
WILSON BUILDING'S
DRAMATIC ROTUNDA.

FACING PAGE
ABOVE:
DAYLIGHT STREAMS
IN THROUGH A
SKYLIGHT AT THE TOP
OF THE WILSON
BUILDING'S ROTUNDA.

BELOW:
CITY HALL AS SEEN
THROUGH THE GRID
OF THE WILSON
BUILDING'S ROTUNDA.

THIS PAGE:
A WALKWAY PASSES IN
FRONT OF THE DALZIEL
BUILDING (LEFT),
LEADING PEDESTRIANS
TOWARD THE WILSON
BUILDING ROTUNDA IN
THE DISTANCE.

FACING PAGE
ABOVE:
A MULTI-STORY ATRIUM
DIRECTLY INSIDE THE
DALZIEL BUILDING'S
MAIN ENTRANCE HELPS
TO ORIENT VISITORS.

BELOW LEFT:
THE DESIGN FOR THE
DALZIEL BUILDING
INCORPORATES INSET
PANELS AND
ORNAMENTATION
THAT RECALL THE
AREA'S HISTORIC
ARCHITECTURE.

BELOW RIGHT:
THE DALZIEL BUILDING'S
MULTI-STORY LOBBY
BECOMES TRANSPARENT
AT NIGHT, ALLOWING
PASSERS-BY TO VIEW
THE INTERIOR.

like many of the nation's government facilities. The Fentress Bradburn team incorporated intricately detailed bases because of high public visibility, while leaving the middle section rather plain and unanimated. However, the highly decorative top section brings closure to the up-sweeping walls and establishes the buildings' prominence from a distance. Beyond applying the tripartite design to these new facilities, the firm established clear circulation paths and inviting open spaces. Additionally, the image of an oak tree was interpreted in the entryway ceiling of the Dalziel Building's lobby to embody the natural environ-

ment of Oakland. While the new facilities meld with the campus' pre-existing buildings, their innovative designs and functional aspects set them apart as civic structures for the 21st century.

The scale of the buildings parallels that of the surrounding structures. The new buildings incorporate elements of traditional civic architecture. Variation in the exterior precast colors helps the building embody the architecture of the early 1900s. In addition, the new buildings' minimal brick details reference the area's historic architecture.

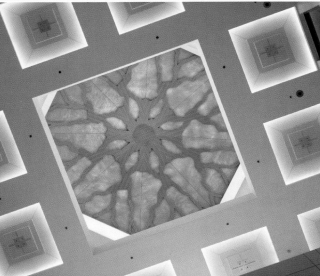

A warm, though neutral, color palette creates harmony with the city and sets a standard for future development in the area. Long façades reduce the visual mass of the building, while echoing the historic buildings of Oakland. Furthermore, key design features, such as entrances, are clearly articulated through atriums, making them easy to find and access. In essence, the buildings and the plaza help revive Oakland's city life by re-weaving the city's urban fabric. The designs visually and physically consolidate the city government's operational needs and turn a once-confusing complex into one that users can easily navigate.

The new Frank H. Ogawa Plaza is a centrally located public gathering place that connects to various public functions. In conjunction with the Wilson Building, the plaza was designed to emphasize City Hall's historic prominence. The scale and massing of the new structures were carefully planned. Colors and palette materials used in the City Hall were replicated in the plaza to unify the character of the entire government complex. The Dalziel Building's entry lobby stands out as a grand "front parlor" for Oakland citizens. Clearly visible, the plaza creates linkages to the government center as well as surrounding neighborhoods and activities.

The character and detailing of the buildings' exteriors are sympathetic to the neighboring architecture. Their entrances are appropriately scaled and clearly located to accommodate the flow of visitors. Overall, the plaza functions as an outdoor living room for citizens by expanding the area westward, to Clay Street, and increasing the emphasis placed on City Hall. Entries into this large open area are highly visible and encourage pedestrian movement and active gatherings. The plaza will entertain theater, concert and parade activities as well as art fairs, dances and political events. The Percent for Art program provided funding for the display of several works of art, further enhancing the rich experience for plaza users.

Fentress Bradburn's overall design for the city administration buildings and plaza centralizes city offices and functions that were previously dispersed throughout Oakland. The new buildings also form a unique and distinct landmark in the heart of the city. Fentress Bradburn's functional urban design is helping to revitalize a downtown that was devastated by natural disaster.

FACING PAGE:
THOSE FUNCTIONS WITH THE GREATEST PUBLIC CONTACT ARE LOCATED ON THE BUILDING'S FIRST FEW FLOORS AND ARE EASILY ACCESSIBLE FROM THE LOBBY.

THIS PAGE
ABOVE: DIRECTIONAL PATTERNS USED ON THE FLOOR HELP DIRECT VISITORS TO ELEVATORS.

CENTER:
AN ABSTRACT OAK TREE, SYMBOL OF THE CITY, ADORNS THE CEILING OF THE DALZIEL BUILDING'S LOBBY.

BELOW:
COLUMNAR FORMS EVOKE THE DIGNITY OF CIVIC STRUCTURES.

DAVID E. SKAGGS FEDERAL BUILDING

BOULDER, COLORADO

The new David E. Skaggs Federal Building was commissioned by the General Services Administration (GSA) to serve as the headquarters building for the National Oceanic and Atmospheric Administration's Boulder Research Group. The building flanks the majestic Flatiron Mountains west of Boulder, Colorado.

The facility houses many diverse tenants with specialized needs and accommodates all of the 1,035 NOAA employees in the Boulder area, who were previously divided between two campuses. Included in the plan were a 372,000-square-foot building, a 600-car parking area, ample bike-lock space, a solar observatory, an antenna farm and field research trailer pads. In the January 1996 issue of *Architecture* magazine, the GSA identified this state-of-the-art research and office facility as a prototype for new federal architecture.

The facility is designed to meet the sophisticated needs of various divisions, including the Environmental Research Laboratories, the region's National Weather Service Forecast Office and the National Geophysical Data Center. The building's 698 offices, twenty conference rooms, 98 laboratories and three major computer centers utilize space effectively and logically. Laboratories and automated data-processing spaces are generally located internally; office spaces line the perimeter. Fentress Bradburn's design allows employees to enjoy the spectacular mountain views. The transom windows located above exterior office

doorways bring light into the interior hallways. All of the exterior windows are operable, allowing the favorable weather conditions of Boulder to provide fresh air for its users nearly year-round.

Energy conservation and environmental sensitivity were major concerns for both the client and the architects. These concerns were addressed with a diverse array of advanced systems. The Skaggs facility is the first building the GSA has built in the region that exceeds mandatory energy-conservation performance standards for new federal buildings.

One of the most interesting energy-saving measures is based on the building's irregular usage patterns. Motion sensors were installed to help track usage and determine the energy needs within various spaces. This type of monitoring greatly minimizes energy expenditures in buildings with non-uniform occupancies, which are typical in this facility. For example, depending on the presence of people in an office or lab, the system knows whether to feed warm or cold air into the space to stabilize its temperature, dim or shut off lights or minimize energy used by certain equipment. The facility's cast-in-place concrete frame minimizes the vibration potential, which could impact research performance. Laboratory floors are finished in concrete, a material chosen for its ability to control vibrations and its impermeability to water and chemical spills. The labs are also well-suited to handle high-pressure gases, toxic or

THIS PAGE:
THIS ASHLAR-STONE BUILDING FLANKS THE MAJESTIC FLATIRON MOUNTAINS WEST OF BOULDER, COLORADO.

FACING PAGE:
THIS FACILITY SERVES AS THE HEADQUARTERS FOR THE NATIONAL OCEANIC AND ATMOSPHERIC ADMINISTRATION'S BOULDER RESEARCH GROUP.

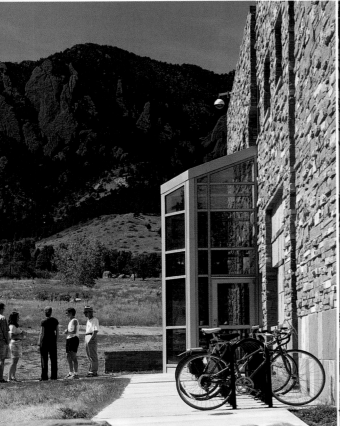

FACING PAGE:
THE SLEEK LINES OF
THE ALUMINUM-AND-
GLASS ENTRYWAY
SPEAK OF THE
SCIENTIFIC CULTURE
WITHIN THE BUILDING.

THIS PAGE
ABOVE:
ON PORTIONS OF THE
CURVED SECTION OF
THE BUILDING'S WEST
FAÇADE, THE
ARCHITECTURAL
PRE-CAST CONCRETE IS
INLAID WITH RIBBONS
OF SANDSTONE.

BELOW LEFT:
THE SIDE ENTRANCE,
CONSTRUCTED
OF ALUMINUM-AND-
GLASS, PUNCTUATES
AN ASHLAR-
STONE WALL.

BELOW RIGHT:
A SANDSTONE FIN
PROJECTS FROM ONE
OF THE ALUMINUM-AND-
GLASS STAIRWELLS.

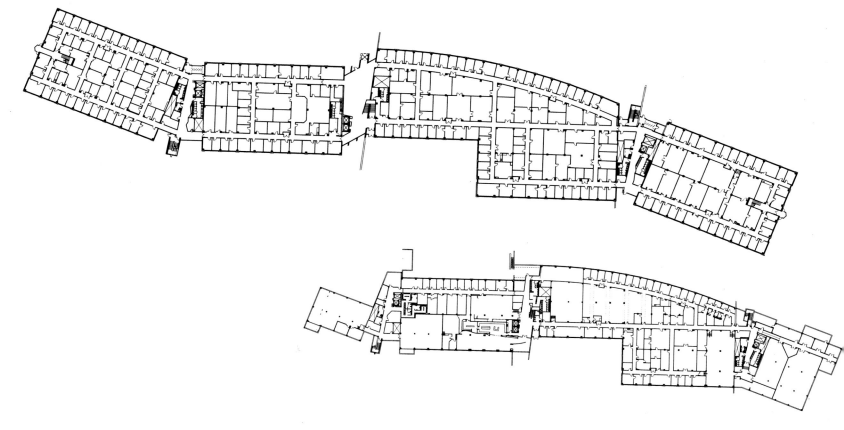

irritating chemicals and high voltages that research in the facility requires.

THIS PAGE
ABOVE:
THE FLOOR PLAN
FOR LEVEL THREE (TOP)
AND THE GARDEN
LEVEL (BELOW). THE
DESIGN ENSURES THAT
THE USERS WILL BE
ABLE TO ENJOY THE
BEAUTIFUL NATURAL
ENVIRONMENT.
THE FLOOR PLANS
GENERALLY LOCATE
LABORATORIES AND
AUTOMATED DATA-
PROCESSING SPACES
INTERNALLY, RESERVING
THE PERIMETER
OF THE BUILDING FOR
OFFICE SPACE.

RIGHT:
THE DISTINCTIVE METAL
RAINDROP RAILING
ABOVE THE ENTRANCE
IS SEEN AGAINST THE
FLATIRON MOUNTAINS.

FACING PAGE:
THE LOBBY FEATURES
A HALF-SIZED SATELLITE
REPLICA (TOP) AND
A KINETIC SCULPTURE
(BOTTOM). THE
ARTICULATED METAL
BALUSTRADE IS
CONTINUOUS FROM
THE EXTERIOR OF
THE BUILDING.

An aesthetically driven design, an awareness of community issues and a respect for the area's striking natural landscape all shaped the building. The design divides the research center into four staggered blocks with three curtain-walled cores that house stairwells and elevators, thereby imitating the structure's Flatiron Mountain backdrop. Fentress Bradburn's sensitivity to exterior and interior environments links the architecture and interior design of this facility to prominent civic buildings. The flooring in the lobby features a rainbow granite that mimics cloud formations, evoking the facility's scientific functions, while the outside of the building is clad with native stone quarried in nearby Lyons, Colorado, and pre-cast concrete panels in matching colors.

Fentress Bradburn established elevation with the fluid placement of windows and clerestory entrances in the Colorado flagstone. The exterior, predominantly Colorado rose and buff sandstones, helps give the building a personal and pedestrian feeling by minimizing its perceived mass.

After attending many meetings with the community and the users, Fentress Bradburn designed a building that not only sits 900 feet west of the closest thoroughfare and 400 feet from the nearest neighborhood, but also preserves sight lines to the magnificent Flatirons and the Rocky Mountains beyond. By dropping the first level below grade, the architects afford area residents continued enjoyment of the site's park-like qualities.

THE BUILDING
WAS PROVIDED WITH
RAISED-FLOOR ACCESS
TO COMPUTER,
TELECOMMUNICATIONS
AND ELECTRICAL
AND MECHANICAL
FUNCTIONS.

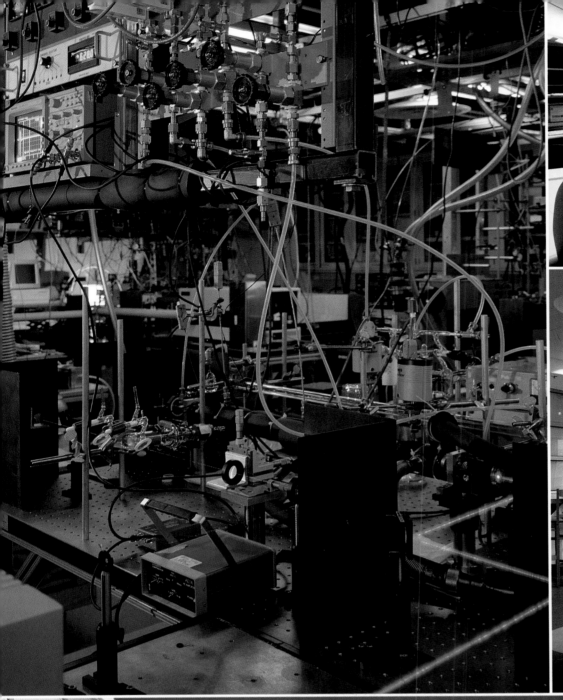

ABOVE LEFT:
LASER BEAMS LIGHT
UP A LABORATORY.

ABOVE RIGHT:
SOLAR FLARES ARE
MONITORED IN ONE OF
NOAA'S LABS.

CENTER RIGHT:
THE CAFETERIA
FEATURES A COUNTER
(RIGHT) WITH
BARSTOOLS FOR
SINGLE DINERS.

BELOW:
A TECHNICIAN CHECKS
THE EQUIPMENT
AMID A CLUSTER OF
OBSERVATORY DOMES
ON THE FACILITY'S ROOF.

CLARK COUNTY GOVERNMENT CENTER

CLARK COUNTY, NEVADA

Clark County's desire to create a service-oriented government center near "The Strip" in Las Vegas, Nevada, inspired the construction of this new building. The Clark County General Services Department held a national design competition and awarded first place to Fentress Bradburn for a design solution that approached the county's requirements sensitively and creatively.

Firmly rooted in its natural setting, the 350,000-square-foot, four-building complex consists of a six-story county administration building and three single-story buildings that house the County Commissioners chambers, a multi-purpose community facility and a central plant. In order to create a symbol of civic order, the architects arranged all functions of the complex in clusters around a central courtyard. The design is logical, functional and straightforward. It establishes a sense of place by using one of the oldest forms of community geometry—the circle. The inviting outstretched arms of the building's semi-circular design symbolize openness and accessibility while functioning as a way-finding device for visitors. Fentress Bradburn's approach and design give the Clark County Government Center a sense of stability and permanence.

The architects used a central courtyard to complete the buildings' circular form and promote an increased sense of community pride and interaction. The courtyard is lined with a pedestrian spine and three rows of trees that frame a grassy sloped amphitheater. A raised platform in the center of the 1.5-acre, 280-foot-diameter amphitheater functions as a stage capable of accommodating almost any type of major public gathering, theatrical production or public ceremony. The central location of the amphitheater reflects the spiritual center of the community. It symbolizes the social aspects of private life and emphasizes the openness and accessibility of government for all. Radial alignment of columns and trees creates a feeling of civic order and a natural outdoor setting for community activities.

Clark County's striking landscape and natural environment inspired the design for the new government center and its courtyard. Using natural materials and forms unique to Clark County, the architects related the building to its

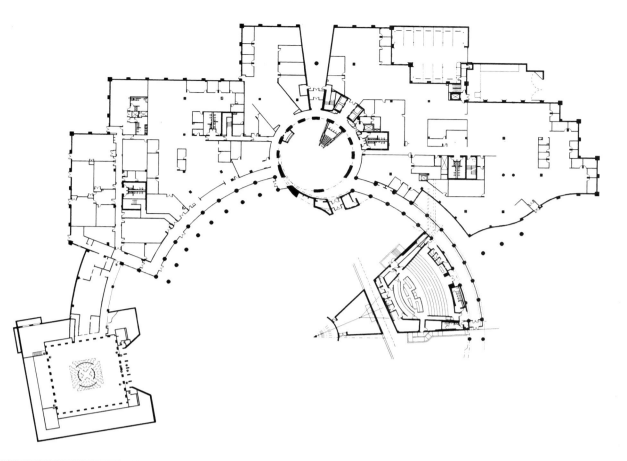

LEFT:
THE FIRST FLOOR
PLAN ILLUSTRATES
HOW THE TRIANGULAR
COMMISSIONER'S
CHAMBER (RIGHT),
THE ROTUNDA (NEAR
TOP) AND THE PYRAMID
(LOWER LEFT) ARE ALL
ARRANGED AROUND A
CENTRAL COURTYARD.

BELOW:
THE DESERT
SURROUNDING
LAS VEGAS INFORMED
ALL ASPECTS OF
THE DESIGN, FROM
THE MOUNTAIN-
INSPIRED PYRAMID TO
THE CANYON-LIKE
APPROACH AND ROTUNDA.

FACING PAGE:
THE INVITING
OUTSTRETCHED ARMS
OF THE BUILDING'S
SEMI-CIRCULAR DESIGN
WELCOME VISITORS.

THIS PAGE
ABOVE LEFT:
THE DENSE FORMS
AND RICH HUES FOUND
THROUGHOUT THE
COMPLEX REFLECT THE
NATURAL CONTEXT.

ABOVE RIGHT:
THE SIMPLE DESIGN
AND BUILDING
ELEMENTS EXUDE AN
ETERNAL PRESENCE
THROUGH THEIR
STRONG, DIGNIFIED
APPEARANCE.

LEFT:
THE COMPLEX IS
ARRANGED AROUND A
CIRCULAR COURTYARD
THAT IS USED FOR
CONCERTS AND OTHER
GATHERINGS.

ABOVE:
THE PYRAMID BUILDING
INCORPORATES SLOTTED
SKYLIGHTS, DESIGNED
IN AN UNUSUAL
CURVILINEAR SHAPE,
TO PROVIDE THE SPACE
WITH DAYLIGHT.

RIGHT:
THE SKYLIGHTS CONNECT
THE BUILDING WITH THE
NATURAL ENVIRONMENT,
GIVING VISITORS A
GLIMPSE OF SKY FROM
INSIDE THE PYRAMID.

ABOVE LEFT:
TRIANGULAR
CLERESTORIES ON THE
ROOF OF THE
COMMISSIONER'S
CHAMBER FLOOD THE
INTERIOR WITH LIGHT
BY DAY AND GLOW
FROM WITHIN AT NIGHT.

ABOVE:
A SHADED
ARCADE COMPLETES
THE CIRCULAR
CONFIGURATION OF
THE COMPLEX.

LEFT:
THE PYRAMID
BUILDING ECHOES
THE PEAKS OF ITS
MOUNTAIN BACKDROP.

ABOVE LEFT:
THE SIX-STORY LOBBY
ROTUNDA EMULATES
THE "POTHOLE"
CANYONS OF THE
REGION, WHICH OFFER
SHELTER FROM THE
DESERT SUN.

ABOVE RIGHT:
A SHADING DEVICE
AFFIXED TO THE
SKYLIGHT AT THE TOP
OF THE ROTUNDA
SERVES TO SCREEN
THE HARSH DESERT
SUNLIGHT.

RIGHT:
THE DESIGN TEAM
USED MOSTLY OPEN
FLOOR PLANS TO
PROVIDE FLEXIBILITY.

surroundings and created an overall sense of belonging. The dense forms and rich natural hues found throughout the center reflect the richness of its natural context; the simple design and building elements exude an eternal presence through their strong, dignified appearance.

Landscaping around the courtyard was planned as a cooling device that would offer refuge from the harsh desert climate and encourage outdoor public events. In this case, landscaping meets environmental and practical needs, while also satisfying the functional and aesthetic needs of the structure. In this area, the architects provided spaces for walking, sitting, eating, talking and performing.

The program required that the space be cost-effective but still meet the challenges of growth and redevelopment. Considering that 60 percent of Nevada's residents live in Clark County, and approximately 5,000 people per month were moving to Las Vegas in 1994, expansion capability was an absolute must for the new government center.

The functional components of the structure are flexible enough to accommodate future expansion without compromising the integrity of the original courtyard form. To extend this flexibility into the office environments, the design team used mostly open floor plans. Offices requiring privacy were placed around the perimeter and divided with demountable floor-to-ceiling partitions. Clerestories were designed to provide interior daylighting. Multi-functional cast-in-place boxes, containing ports for power, communication and data, as well as a separate circuit for isolated ground power, were placed on a grid system compatible with the furniture system. Standardized beam penetrations and flexible lighting connections allow for easy and convenient relocation of mechanical and electrical systems in the future. To increase communication and data accessibility, cable trays were utilized for horizontal distribution of the fiber-optic backbone to numerous vertical distribution cores.

ABOVE:
THE LOBBY'S SCULPTURAL LAMPS WERE FASHIONED AFTER DESERT BLOSSOMS AND THE TOUGH VINES THAT SUSTAIN THEM. THEY ARE SEEN HERE AGAINST THE SKYLIGHT SCREEN ON THE ROTUNDA'S CEILING.

LEFT:
TRIANGULAR CLERESTORIES IN THE CEILING OF THE COMMISSIONER'S CHAMBER FLOOD THE INTERIOR WITH LIGHT AND CONTINUE THE IMAGERY OF CACTUS SPINES.

REGIONAL TRANSPORTATION COMMISSION and REGIONAL FLOOD CONTROL DISTRICT HEADQUARTERS

CLARK COUNTY, NEVADA

Using a materials palette similar to that of the Clark County Government Center, the architects designed a second building as part of the master plan for the 38-acre Clark County campus. The Regional Transportation Commission and Regional Flood Control District Headquarters and Administrative Center (RTC/RFCD) are considered semi-public in nature when compared to the government center. Natural sandstone on the exterior of the building complements the natural landforms of the region and the adjacent government center. The building's design was inspired by Nevada's native landscapes, found at Red Rock Canyon and Valley of Fire, and thus reflects Fentress Bradburn's design philosophy of contextual regionalism.

The main entrance is accessed by a central courtyard on the south side of the building. Shaded by high building masses on the east and west side, the courtyard appears to be surrounded by high canyon walls; patrons feel as if they

FACING PAGE:
THE CURVILINEAR WALLS, WHICH SLOPE OUTWARD FROM THE BASE, CREATE A SPATIAL EXPERIENCE SIMILAR TO THAT INSIDE A CANYON.

THIS PAGE
BELOW:
SEEN FROM THE SOUTH, THE BUILDING'S WALLS RISE UP AROUND THE COURTYARD.

are walking through a desert canyon. In order to replicate a canyon and create a similar spatial experience, the architects used curvilinear walls that slope outward from the base of the building in an asymmetrical order. Landscape design reinforces the canyon references with a palette of colors, materials, textures and plants inspired by a desert atmosphere.

Many energy-saving features were incorporated into the facility. Maximum use of natural light and low-energy supplementary lighting control systems are offset by highly efficient, insulated "low-E" tinted and coated glass that controls solar gain and radiant heat transfer. Use of pedestrian arcades on the east and south face of the building also prevents excess heat gain while providing a pleasant approach to the building. Three continuous rows of trees, called Pine Allée, run along the west face of the building, providing shade from the afternoon sun.

Combined, the Clark County Government Center and the RTC/RFCD Headquarters and Administrative Center provide the public with a space that is not only highly functional and efficient but inviting and architecturally distinctive.

THIS PAGE
RIGHT:
THE CURVING WALLS
CREATE DRAMATIC
FORMS THAT RELATE
THE BUILDING
TO ITS CONTEXT.

CENTER:
WINDOWS OF DIFFERENT
SIZES AND SHAPES
ARE PARTIALLY
RECESSED, ECHOING
THE IRREGULAR
OPENINGS FOUND IN A
CANYON SETTING.

FACING PAGE
ABOVE:
AN ARCADE ALONG
THE EAST FAÇADE
SHELTERS VISITORS
FROM THE SUN AS
THEY NAVIGATE THE
COMPLEX.

BELOW:
THE LOBBY IS LIT
BY DIRECT SUN
AT MIDDAY, WHEN
SUNLIGHT IS NOT
SCREENED OFF BY
THE STRUCTURE'S
"CANYON" WALLS.

JEFFERSON COUNTY COURTS and ADMINISTRATION BUILDING

GOLDEN, COLORADO

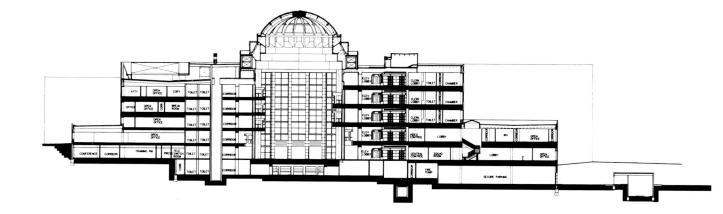

THIS PAGE
RIGHT:
BUILDING ELEVATION.

BELOW:
AN AERIAL VIEW OF
THE BUILDING'S
SOUTHWEST FAÇADE
ILLUSTRATES THE
CIRCUITOUS
APPROACH, WHICH
MINIMIZES ITS MASS.

FACING PAGE:
THE TWO MAIN ARCS
OF THE BUILDING
ARE CONNECTED BY
THE ENTRYWAY'S
SOARING ROTUNDA.

The consolidation of numerous governmental departments into one centralized welcoming space was the major requirement for Jefferson County's government center, located in Golden, Colorado. Fentress Bradburn's timeless design of the 531,000-square-foot facility affords expansion capabilities for the next 20 years. The judicial wing of the structure comprises 304,000 square feet, while the administrative wing, joined by the central lobby atrium, utilizes the remaining 227,000 square feet. Concealed either underground or by artful landscaping, the government center's two-story parking structure holds 1,400 vehicles and serves both wings. In addition, a new 15,000-square-foot underground tunnel and central holding facility connects the judicial building to a pre-existing detention center.

Fentress Bradburn's master plan for the 180-acre campus was designed to give the quickly growing rural and suburban county, west of Denver, a seat of government that

LARIMER COUNTY JUSTICE CENTER

FORT COLLINS, COLORADO

As part of its downtown Fort Collins redevelopment program, Larimer County, Colorado, held a design competition for the Larimer County Justice Center, a 170,000-square-foot facility. Fentress Bradburn's design was picked out of three national design-build proposals because it best met the county's goals. The five-story design, which accommodates spaces that will be functional well into the future, maximizes the efficiency of the court's program, facilitates future use and expansion and maintains open public areas. The project includes spaces for office, retail, recreation and parking. The courthouse itself is designed to reinforce the Civic Center master plan by providing pedestrian-scaled public spaces within multiple interconnecting blocks. Departments are positioned within the five stories according to the volume of public access required. Departments with

the least public access are located on upper levels, while those departments that have a great deal of public visitation are situated in the lower floors.

The courthouse is located on the northeast corner of the block, across from the 900-car Civic Center Parking Structure. This building is also part of the Civic Center's master plan, which promotes the development of mixed-use civic projects. Primary entrances for both buildings are located at the corners to reinforce the urban design characteristics and traditions of Fort Collins. Each of these projects encourages pedestrian-scaled street frontages; the design of each is sensitive to the historical context of two- and four-story brick commercial buildings. Alignment of the traditional corner entrance with the street edge honors the other tra-

THIS PAGE:
THIS 170,000-
SQUARE-FOOT
JUSTICE CENTER
WAS BUILT AS
A PART OF
FORT COLLINS' REDE-
VELOPMENT
PROGRAM.

FACING PAGE:
PRIMARY ENTRANCES
WERE LOCATED AT
STREET CORNERS
TO REINFORCE THE
URBAN DESIGN
CHARACTERISTICS
AND TRADITIONS
OF FORT COLLINS.

ditional buildings set to the property line and creates a rich street-front experience. The master plan also incorporates a series of public spaces linked by a mid-block pedestrian spine that encompasses the entire Civic Center district, ending at Lee Martinez Park and the Poudre River to the north.

The architects decided on massing and exterior materials that reinforce the civic and urban nature of the project. Lower levels are aligned with the street edge, while the upper three floors are set back from the street so that a historic scale is maintained and abundant natural light can reach the street. Exterior building materials include sandstone and brick organized in a pattern that reinforces the two-story base component of the building and expresses the brick pilaster and arcade configuration common to the area. The courthouse's configuration allows winter sun to penetrate into Civic Center Park.

Three separate circulation routes for the public, court staff and prisoners are clearly laid out. Public entries to the courts are located on the southwest and northeast sides. Security checkpoints consist of walk-through magnetometers and package x-ray machines. The public circulation route has a separate and distinct exit to ensure the safety of occupants and visitors. The public corridor connects patrons to all courtrooms, departmental reception spaces and the judges' reception areas.

A main public plaza, southwest of the courthouse, overlooks a park and doubles as a forecourt for the building and an amphitheater for small lunchtime performances or community gatherings. Fentress Bradburn designed the fountain as the central feature of the plaza. It constitutes the largest portion of the public art program and symbolizes a balance between community partnership and individual rights. Incorporating accessible outdoor spaces for building users is a key component of Fentress Bradburn's work, because of its humanizing effect.

The Larimer County Justice Center currently contains 14 courtrooms; the facility has the capacity to expand and accommodate three additional courtrooms. The site area has been preserved for long-term expansion to the west, to accommodate nearly double the number of courtrooms, if needed. To minimize disruption and simplify security and user interaction, the initial secured entrances and elevator core will continue to serve as the primary circulation paths for the future courthouse expansion.

FACING PAGE:
THE FIVE-STORY JUSTICE CENTER WAS ORGANIZED SO THAT THOSE OFFICES WITH THE MOST PUBLIC CONTACT WERE LOCATED ON THE LOWEST FLOORS.

THIS PAGE
LEFT:
THE LARIMER COUNTY JUSTICE CENTER CONTAINS 14 COURTROOMS; THE FACILITY CAN EXPAND TO ACCOMMODATE THREE ADDITIONAL COURTROOMS.

RIGHT:
LOWER LEVELS ARE ALIGNED WITH THE STREET EDGE, WHILE THE THREE UPPER LEVELS ARE SET BACK SO THAT A HISTORIC SCALE IS MAINTAINED AND ABUNDANT LIGHT CAN REACH THE STREET.

CIVIC CENTER PARKING STRUCTURE
FORT COLLINS, COLORADO

THE PARKING
GARAGE IS A FOUR-
LEVEL STRUCTURE,
WHICH PROVIDES
15,000 SQUARE
FEET OF RETAIL
SPACE ALONG THE
STREET LEVEL.

In order to accommodate the large volume of people using the new courthouse, Fentress Bradburn completed plans for a Civic Center Parking Structure. The parking garage is a four-level structure with a 900-vehicle capacity and an additional 15,000 square feet of retail space along the street level. The architects related the overall design of the parking structure to the look and feel of existing retail storefronts along Mason Street. Their plan transformed the bulk and mass of the parking garage into a turn-of-the-century masonry structure that matched the surrounding architecture.

A recessed window aesthetic is used throughout the structure to provide continuity with the rectangular window proportions used in adjacent buildings. Window propor-

tions, as well as enclosure detailing found in the courthouse, harmonize with the look of the street level retail functions to assure that the building fits seamlessly into its context. Although signage clearly delineates the garage as a parking facility, the structure defies the usual parking ramp "box" and blends easily with its surroundings. Vehicular access is provided from both Mason Street on the west and LaPorte Street on the north. A flow-through design was utilized to minimize congestion while maximizing flexibility of use and maintaining clear separation between vehicular and pedestrian pathways.

ABOVE:
THE ARCHITECTS RELATED THE OVERALL DESIGN OF THE PARKING STRUCTURE TO THE LOOK AND FEEL OF EXISITING RETAIL STOREFRONTS ALONG MASON STREET.

LEFT:
THE THREE-LANE ENTRYWAY CAN BE RE-CONFIGURED TO ACCOMMODATE A TWO-LANE EGRESS OR INGRESS, DEPENDING ON THE FACILITY'S NEEDS.

AIRPORTS

"The experience of using an airport should be more than simply catching a plane. Yes, the building should function flawlessly and make it easy to accomplish one's purpose, but the airport should be symbolic of its city or region—it should be a gateway. This symbolism should create a presence that greets the traveler."

- Curt Fentress

TOP LEFT:
DAYLIGHT POURS
IN THROUGH
CLERESTORIES IN THE
TERMINAL'S CEILING.

TOP RIGHT:
ENOUGH LIGHT
PENETRATES THE
GREAT HALL TO
SUPPORT TRADITIONAL
KOREAN GARDENS.

ABOVE:
MASTS ATOP THE
BUILDING REFER TO
SHIPS IN NEARBY
INCHON HARBOR AND
CONNECT THE AIRPORT
TO ITS CONTEXT.

LEFT:
THE FLUID WAVE-LIKE
FORM OF THE
TERMINAL'S ROOF
REFERENCES WATER,
AS WELL AS THE
AERODYNAMIC SHAPE
OF AIRCRAFT.

FACING PAGE
ABOVE:
SKYLIGHTS OVER
THE CONCOURSE
PROVIDE ABUNDANT
SUNLIGHT DURING
THE DAY, REDUCING
THE NEED FOR
ARTIFICIAL LIGHTING.

BELOW:
THE ARTICULATED
FRAME OF THE
TICKETING HALL
FOLLOWS THE CURVE
OF THE BUILDING.

THIS PAGE:
THE WAVE-LIKE FORM
OF THE ROOF IS
ECHOED BY THE
DESIGN OF INTERIOR
LAMPS, SEEN HERE AT
THE TERMINAL'S GLASS
CURTAIN WALL.

The exterior of the main terminal represents a juxtaposition of earth and sky in much the same way that the roof symbolizes air and water. Fentress Bradburn used textured concrete materials to ground the lower two levels of the structure. In contrast, the concourse and departure halls of the upper level employ glass and steel to create a feeling of air and sky. The airport improves circulation flow and orientation by embracing and welcoming passengers through the curved forms of the terminal structure. The curve of the main terminal also unifies the circulation spaces from end to end, allowing passengers to navigate quickly and easily. Although the length of the terminal is almost three-quarters of a mile, a series of people movers insures that users will not walk any distances greater than 400 feet. At ultimate development, four satellite island concourses will provide 128 additional wide-body gates to the facility, bringing the total to 174 and accommodating 100 million passengers per year.

The architects arranged concourse floors and terminal interiors thematically, employing historical Korean images of earth, sky and water. The platform serving the intra-airport transit and people-mover systems is inlaid with blue granite, symbolizing water and evoking images of movement. Green granite, representing plants and trees, is used in the arrivals level, which serves as a welcoming area for travelers. Ticketing and concourse areas, located on the departures level, are detailed with gold granite, a reference to harvested plants. Gold was also chosen for its calming influence on passengers. The walls and ceilings of the interior are painted in a light neutral palette that illuminates the space and exudes an airy quality; the floors, finished in a medium-toned palette, ground the spaces.

Fentress Bradburn also used images of the tiger and the dragon in the design. Korea has emerged as a major force in global trade and commerce and many people now view it as one of the "tigers" of Asia. The use of tiger and dragon patterns also reiterates the earth and sky dichotomy present throughout the building. The mythical and mystical dragon symbolizes air and flight; the tiger, used to symbolize earth, is rendered in an organic, symmetrical pattern throughout the landside area of the airport terminal. The Fentress Bradburn team also makes the space more intimate by utilizing small-scale dragon and tiger patterns.

ABOVE RIGHT:
A RAILED SHADING DEVICE TOPS THE GLASS CURTAIN WALL AT ONE END OF THE MAIN TERMINAL. THE GLASS IS HELD IN PLACE BY A CABLE-TRUSS SYSTEM THAT CURVES OUT FROM THE WALL.

BELOW RIGHT:
SITE MODEL. INCHON HARBOR APPEARS IN THE FOREGROUND; THE TERMINAL IS AT THE TOP.

FACING PAGE:
SHADING DEVICES AT CURBSIDE RESONATE WITH ASIAN BUILDING MOTIFS.

SEATTLE-TACOMA INTERNATIONAL AIRPORT
CENTRAL TERMINAL REDEVELOPMENT
SEATTLE, WASHINGTON

Built in 1947, the central terminal is the airport's oldest structure. The redevelopment and expansion plans for Seattle-Tacoma International Airport not only enhance the original design, but also bring the facility into the next century. As a part of the Port of Seattle's effort to upgrade and renovate the airport, the firm also provided seismic reinforcement in the design.

The Port of Seattle selected Fentress Bradburn from a list of distinguished architects to design the $84 million central terminal redevelopment and expansion at Seattle-Tacoma International Airport in Washington State. The new central terminal has a tall central space, flanked on each side by lower wings and clerestories, a configuration that reiterates the building's original massing. A new 60-foot-tall, 350-foot-long westward-facing glass curtain wall provides travelers panoramic views of the airfield, the Olympic Mountains and Mount Rainier.

To aid passenger way-finding in the building, Fentress Bradburn focused on improving terminal layout and incorporating appropriate signage into interior design, graphic

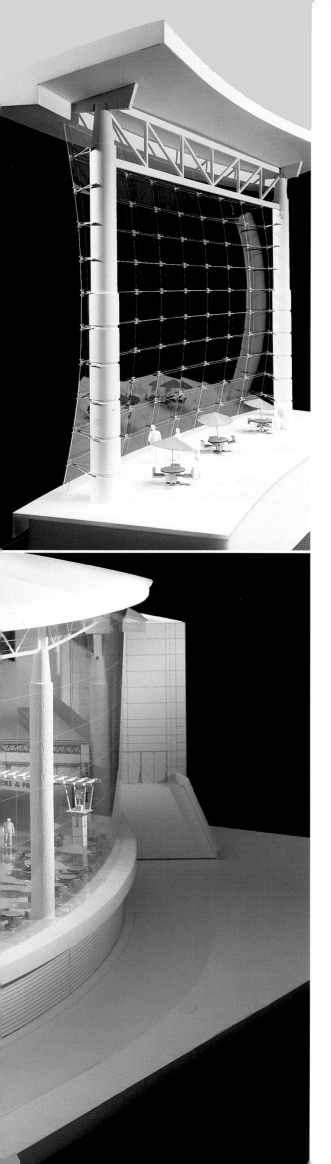

design and landscape architecture. The grand central space is a key design element that functions as an orientation spot, where passengers can find their gates quickly and efficiently. Also included in the central space are retail shops, dining areas and food and beverage facilities. The design increases passenger comfort and convenience by minimizing walking distances and increasing accessibility to retail centers.

The architects took care to represent the Seattle region in their design. The expansive curtain wall system, a tall curved ceiling supported by lightweight trusses, custom light fixtures and granite floors all recall the feeling of Seattle's contemporary outdoor marketplace. Custom light fixtures take the form of outdoor lampposts. Exterior-style metal railings define seating areas; varied storefronts, accented by hanging plants, help to create the image of a downtown marketplace within the central terminal. Each of these details also makes the airport efficient and user-friendly.

To evoke the light and airy feeling of the Northwest, Fentress Bradburn designed the curtain wall, high clerestory windows and round skylights over curved corners to infuse the interior with natural light. In contrast, wood paneling was introduced as the dominant wall treatment, giving the space warmth and richness, qualities that are also reflective of the region.

While creating a new central terminal that would be a landmark facility, both functionally and aesthetically, Fentress Bradburn remained sensitive to the character and design of the existing concourses. Many elements and features from the original 1947 design, such as the custom pre-cast concrete screen design of the old departure gates, are referenced by Art Deco details in the security pavilions. Frit-patterned glass and the fluted stainless steel panels curved over corner skylights are reminiscent of those used on the public elevator jambs and in fascia detailing. The wing design engraved in the security pavilion's glass elements was copied from the terminal's original public elevator doors.

The esplanades were refinished in order to maintain an architecturally consistent look and feel. Retail services and merchandising kiosks, previously located in the center of the building, were relocated to the east wall in order to create the illusion of an extended avenue. A main aisle running between the two streets contains wooden benches, potted trees, additional lampposts and tables with umbrella

ABOVE LEFT:
GLASS USED IN THE NEW CENTRAL TERMINAL CURVES VERTICALLY, AS WELL AS HORIZONTALLY.

LEFT:
THE TERMINAL'S CENTRAL SPACE INCLUDES RETAIL SHOPS AND DINING AREAS .

canopies. Elements such as these enhance the park-like setting created within the central space. The architects maintain continuity by extending the wood-paneled walls, used
throughout the esplanades, into the ticketing hall and the
central terminal.

In addition to the central terminal expansion and redevelopment, Fentress Bradburn also expanded and renovated
Horizon Airlines' facilities for the Port of Seattle. The design
team relocated the outbound baggage system to the newly
expanded area beneath the central terminal, bringing it clos-
er to the airline's ramp operations. Horizon's new hold rooms
on concourses B and C provide better access to ground-
loaded aircraft. The existing ramp level and ground-loaded
commuter-aircraft parking positions were also relocated to
provide 18 additional spaces.

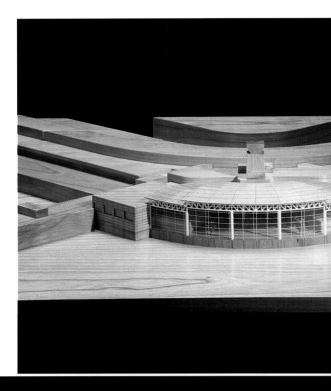

ABOVE RIGHT:
EARLY DESIGN
CONCEPT

RIGHT:
A NEW 60-FOOT-TALL,
350-FOOT-LONG,
WESTWARD-FACING
GLASS CURTAIN WALL
PROVIDES TRAVELERS
WITH PANORAMIC VIEWS
OF THE AIRFIELD, THE
OLYMPIC MOUNTAINS
AND MOUNT RAINIER.

ABOVE LEFT:
VARIED STOREFRONTS
HELP CREATE THE
IMAGE OF A DOWNTOWN
MARKETPLACE WITHIN
THE TERMINAL.

ABOVE RIGHT:
THE TERMINAL'S
CENTRAL SPACE
RECALLS SEATTLE'S
FAMED PIKE
STREET MARKET.

DENVER INTERNATIONAL AIRPORT
PASSENGER TERMINAL COMPLEX
DENVER, COLORADO

Denver International Airport's peaked white roof is an instantly recognizable iconic landmark that welcomes travelers to Colorado. Rising from the semi-arid plains, northeast of downtown Denver, the terminal references the peaks and valleys of its Rocky Mountain backdrop with a jagged roofline.

After years of Stapleton Airport expansions and many complaints from neighboring residential areas about the noise of landings and takeoffs, the decision was made to build a new airport for Denver. To accommodate passenger loads well into the 21st century, the City and County of Denver selected a 53-acre green-field site. Ground was broken on September 28, 1989. During initial grading stages, over 110 million cubic feet of earth were moved—one-third as much earth as was moved during the construction of the Panama Canal. The site was carefully selected to allow for the use of state-of-the-art technologies and a fresh design philosophy that would lend a timeless feel to the overall project. After construction was completed, Fentress Bradburn received the 1995 Design Honor Award from the United States Department of Transportation for its design.

In total, the passenger complex is 1.4 million square feet and can process upwards of 110 million passengers annually. Fentress Bradburn's design also utilizes steel from the fifth floor up, which ultimately allows greater flexibility in accommodating owner-mandated change requests. As a part of the project, the firm also designed a 10-story office building for airport administration and six module parking garages with 12,000 stalls.

The facility has one of the largest structurally-integrated tensile-membrane roofs in the world. Coupled with its striking roof structure, the building's sheer magnitude captivates travelers as they approach from both land and air. The roof structure, held in place by 34 masts that reach as high as 150 feet, can shift up to two feet laterally during high windstorms. Although the roof initially generated some concerns regarding fabric durability, the structure is rated by roofing experts to perform better than conventional roofing

THE TENSILE-MEMBRANE FABRIC ROOF OF DENVER INTERNATIONAL AIRPORT EMULATES THE PEAKS AND VALLEYS OF ITS ROCKY MOUNTAIN BACKDROP.

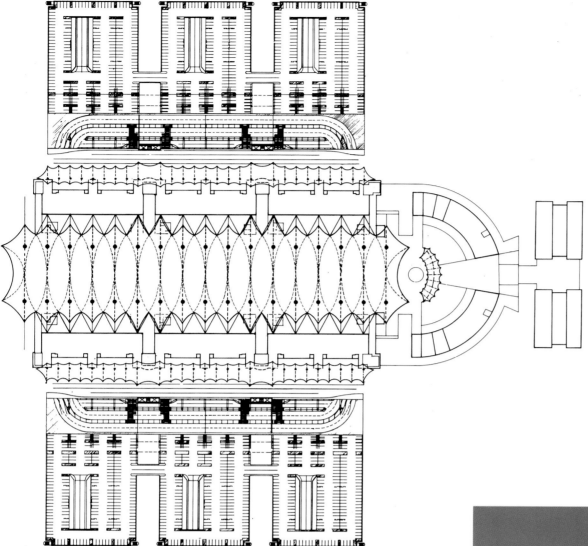

systems for spans greater than 100 feet. The fabric roof weighs two pounds per square foot less than traditional roofing materials. It allows hot air to escape by way of osmosis and minimizes the need for artificial lighting. The roof also reflects 40 percent of incident solar radiation, reducing heat transfer and build-up. Constructed in less than one year and within budget, the roof comes with a warranty that lasts twelve years longer than most conventional roofing systems.

ABOVE:
PARKING GARAGES
FLANK THE TERMINAL
ON THE WEST (TOP)
AND EAST (BOTTOM).

RIGHT:
EIGHT OF THE 34
PEAKS OF THE
TERMINAL'S ROOF ARE
INSET WITH SKYLIGHTS
THAT ALLOW DIRECT
SUNLIGHT TO
PENETRATE INTO
THE GREAT HALL.

The architects took special care to give the airport a calming atmosphere, ensuring that travelers would be comfortable from initial arrival until final departure. Coloradans' enthusiasm for outdoor pursuits and the state's unique climate, which averages 300 days of sunshine per year, are incorporated and reflected in the terminal's exterior and interior design forms. On both sunny and overcast days, natural daylight floods into the space from abundant

clerestories and curtain walls, and through the translucent roof. At night, as the sun sets behind the nearby Rocky Mountains, the roof emits a soft glow and becomes a beacon on the agricultural plains.

The Great Hall is filled with retail shops, cafés and kiosks that create a cosmopolitan environment and respond to the needs of airport users. Comfort, convenience and clear signage translate into shorter walking distances and easy access to ticketing facilities, restrooms, concessions, shops, security areas, train platforms, baggage claims and parking areas. Strategically placed telephone booths, multi-use flight information displays (MUFID's) and park-like seating arrangements divide the space of the airport logically

ABOVE CENTER:
BECAUSE THE ROOF IS NOT RIGID, THE ARCHITECTS HAD TO USE A CABLE-TRUSS SYTEM TO HOLD THE BUILDING'S SOUTH CURTAIN WALL IN PLACE.

ABOVE:
ON BOTH SUNNY AND OVERCAST DAYS, NATURAL DAYLIGHT FLOODS INTO THE SPACE FROM ABUNDANT CLERESTORIES.

BELOW CENTER:
TENSIONING CABLES FOR THE TERMINAL'S ROOF FRAME THE ADMINISTRATIVE OFFICES.

and allow passengers to relax in more intimate spaces. The result is a user-friendly facility that is comfortable, convenient and efficient.

Throughout the interior, the architects used granite floor patterns to establish clear and direct circulation paths for travelers. The patterns mimic the peaks of the tensile roof and the Rocky Mountains, adding another level of cohesiveness to the design. As passengers enter from the curbside drop-off, these patterns beckon them toward ticketing counters and lead them into the Great Hall space. A mixture of granite and carpeting is used in the flooring of the Great Hall's main level. Carpeting in the rest areas reduces the noise level and cushions the soles of weary travelers. An inverted replication of the ticketing hall floor pattern directs arriving passengers from baggage claim out to various forms of ground transportation.

Fentress Bradburn coordinated the efforts of 27 subconsultants, six owner consultants, five contractors, six public artists and twelve government agencies to successfully complete the passenger terminal complex. Senior personnel from the entire team attended weekly Friday meetings from initial concept design through final construction to establish the highest degree of communication and fast, accurate functioning.

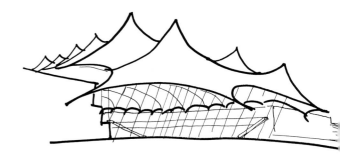

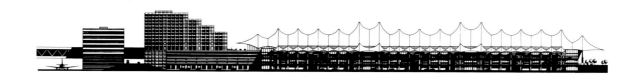

ABOVE:
EARLY SKETCH
OF THE TERMINAL

CENTER:
AS THE SUN SETS
BEHIND THE NEARBY
ROCKY MOUNTAINS,
THE ROOF EMITS
A SOFT GLOW
AND BECOMES A
BEACON ON THE
AGRICULTURAL PLAINS.

RIGHT:
THESE DRAWINGS
ILLUSTRATE A
SECTION (TOP),
THE NORTH FAÇADE
(CENTER) AND
THE WEST FAÇADE
(BOTTOM).

FAR LEFT:
A GRANITE COMPASS ROSE GRACES THE FLOOR OF THE TERMINAL'S TRAIN STATION.

LEFT:
THE SHAPE OF THE LAMPS ON THE FLOOR OF THE TERMINAL (FOREGROUND) IS PATTERNED AFTER THAT OF THE MASTS (BACKGROUND).

BELOW:
FLIGHT INFORMATION DISPLAY MONITORS AT THE NORTH END OF THE GREAT HALL.

THIS PAGE:
THE GREAT HALL
INCORPORATES AN
INTIMATE SEATING
AREA. ELEVATORS
ARE LOCATED IN
THE LARGE COLUMNS
NEAR THE BRIDGE.

FACING PAGE:
A BOW-STRING CABLE-
TRUSS SYSTEM ON THE
INTERIOR HELPS
SUPPORT THE GLASS
CURTAIN WALL ON THE
SOUTHERN FAÇADE.

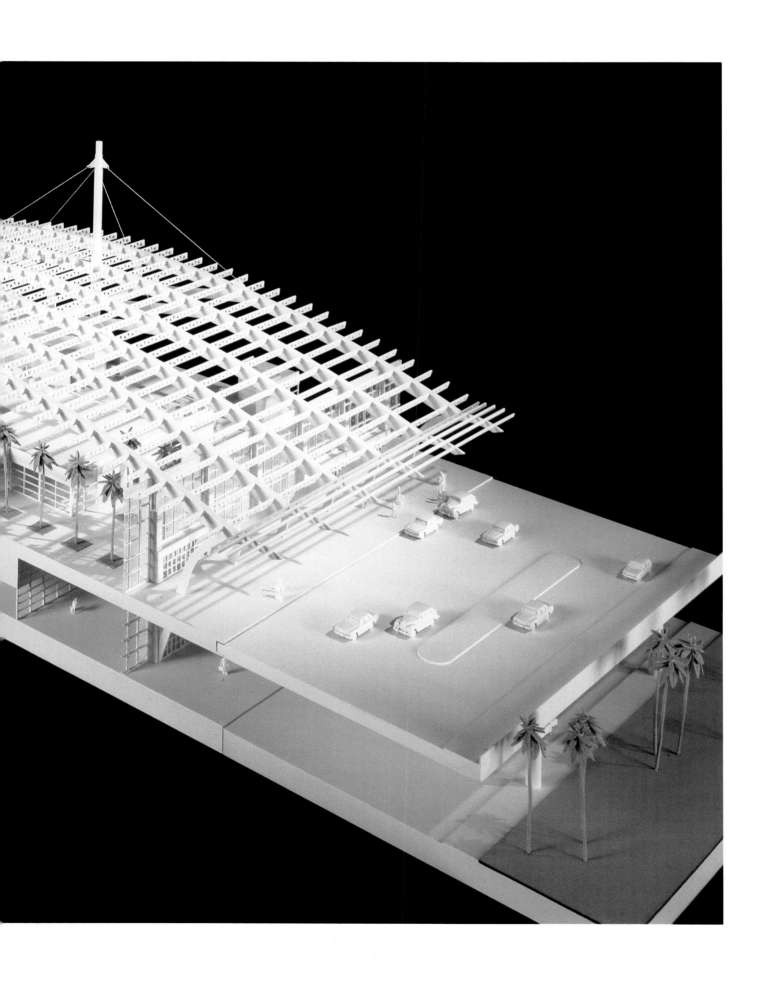

ABOVE:
THE CONTROL
TOWER AND
SUPPORT FACILITIES
INCORPORATE A
WAVE-LIKE PATTERN OF
OPAQUE GLASS WITHIN
THE FENESTRATION.

RIGHT:
THE SOUTH ELEVATION
OF THE FIRE STATION

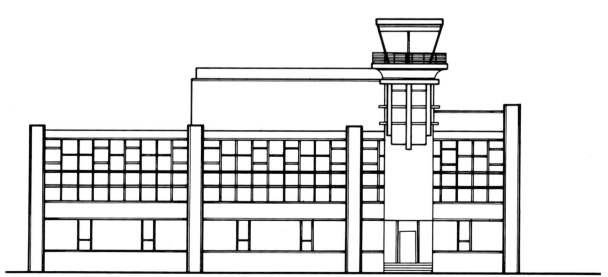

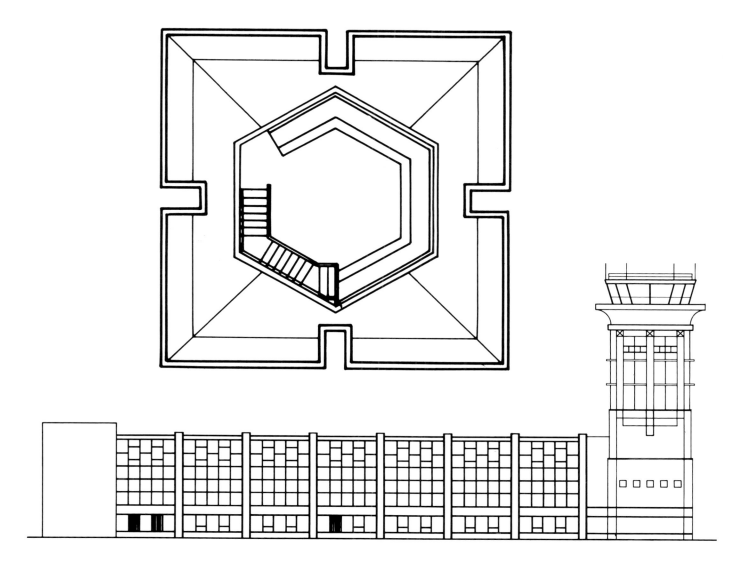

the processing areas, a transfer passenger checkpoint and a hotel for extended-stay transfer travelers. Interstitial space is used for baggage system distribution from the ticket counters, baggage-claim devices and all mechanical, electrical and communication system distribution. All facilities for departing passengers, including the departures hall, security checkpoints, passenger check-in, outbound customs and immigration, retail and concessions, are located on the third level. Level three of the airside concourse contains the departures concourse, holdrooms, retail malls and an airline club.

The region's harsh climate presented challenges during design and construction. Dry, hot and sunny, the desert climate means large cooling costs for any structure. Fentress Bradburn's primary strategy for energy efficiency was to combat heat by cladding the terminal's exterior glass,

including all skylight glazing, with an innovative ceramic frit designed in a traditional Qatari pattern. Cast-in-place and precast white and sand-colored concrete completes the exterior palette, recalling Qatari architectural coloration and the sands of Qatar's great inland desert.

The space is designed to function well into the future, at minimal cost and disturbance to everyday operations. The airport, which will open in 2003 with fourteen attached aircraft gates and twelve hard-stand positions, is capable of expanding to twenty attached aircraft gates and 24 hard-stand positions to fulfill future needs. Ultimate development will allow 10 million passengers to comfortably pass through the airport each year. The firm's extensive airport design experience ensures that Doha International Airport will remain an important global gateway.

TOP:
THE CEILING PLAN OF THE CONTROL TOWER SHOWS STAIRS RISING ALONG THE SOUTHWEST FAÇADE INTO THE OBSERVATION TOWER.

ABOVE:
THIS ELEVATION ILLUSTRATES AN EARLY DESIGN SCHEME FOR THE CONTROL TOWER BUILDING.

VIENNA INTERNATIONAL AIRPORT
TERMINAL COMPLEX EXPANSION — DESIGN COMPETITION
VIENNA, AUSTRIA

Sixteen architects competed for the design of the Vienna International Airport expansion. The program involved doubling the size of the existing terminal and adding 24 aircraft gates, as well as providing a plan for future growth. Fentress Bradburn's design, which won honorable mention, accomplished these programmatic goals and also created a unique image for both Vienna and Austria.

The project was defined by three major physical boundaries: the northwestern edge was bordered by the autobahn; the existing terminal was contained between two operational runways; and new buildings were to be located adjacent to the present airport terminal. Each of these variables posed challenges for the competing architects. In addition, Vienna International Airport's site featured a large variety of building types and identities. By creating a facility that spans the entire site, Fentress Bradburn's design served to unify the site and create a single identity for the individual buildings. The structure floats across the landscape, disrupting nothing, unifying everything, becoming the diameter of a circular approach road that unites the airport with the city plan.

BELOW:
THE NORTHWEST FAÇADE IS SEEN HERE FROM DIFFERENT ANGLES.

RIGHT:
SOUTHWEST FAÇADE; TERMINAL IS WRAPPED IN AN ARTICULATED STEEL CASING.

The airport's expansion involved doubling the terminal's check-in, ticketing and baggage facilities. In order to accomplish these goals in the most efficient and user-friendly

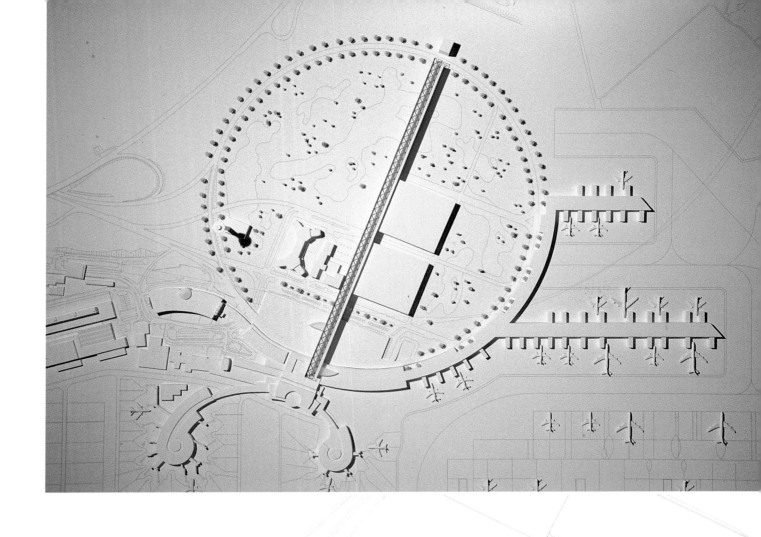

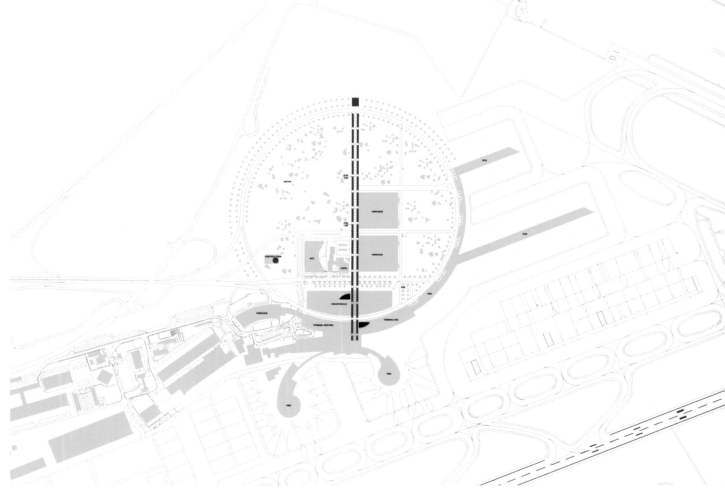

ABOVE:
BY CREATING A
FACILITY THAT SPANS
THE ENTIRE SITE,
FENTRESS BRADBURN'S
DESIGN SERVED
TO UNIFY THE SITE AND
ESTABLISH A SINGLE
IDENTITY FOR THE
INDIVIDUAL BUILDINGS.

RIGHT:
THE SITE PLAN
ILLUSTRATES HOW
THE AIRPORT
CONNECTS WITH THE
NEARBY CITY GRID.
THE AUTOBAHN IS
AT LOWER RIGHT.

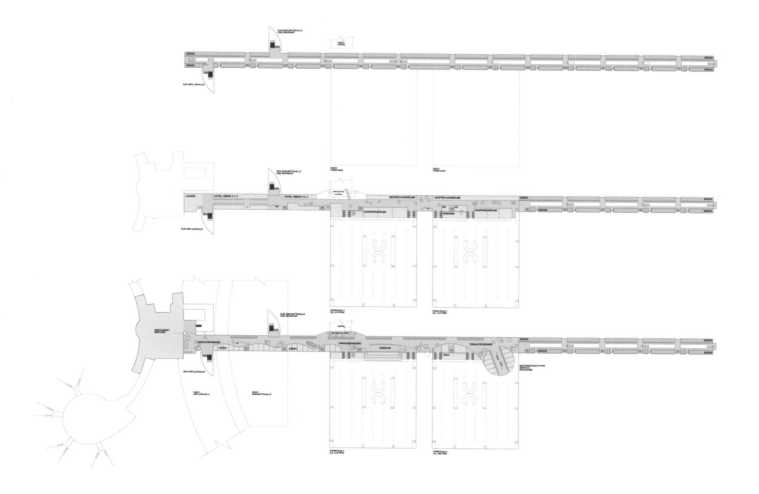

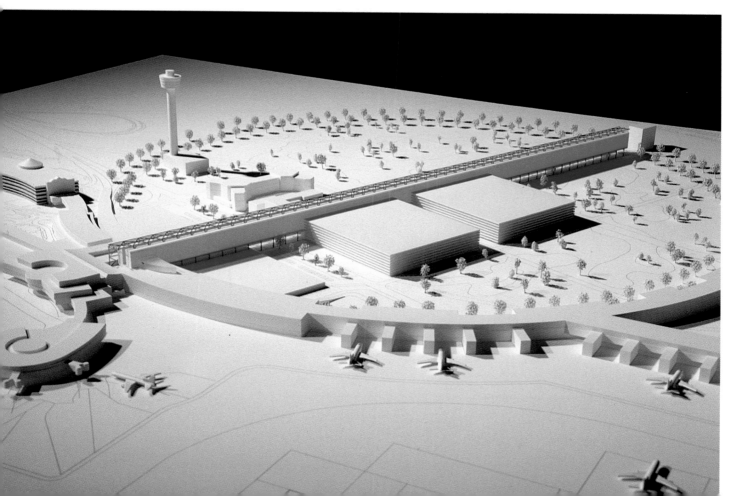

ABOVE:
THE SECOND, FOURTH
AND SIXTH LEVELS.
PLANS SHOW
CONNECTION WITH
PARKING GARAGES AND
EXISTING TERMINAL.

LEFT:
TWO PARKING GARAGES
ARE CONNECTED TO
THE LINEAR TERMINAL.
THE EXISTING
CONCOURSE APPEARS
ON THE LEFT, AND
THE PLANNED
CONCOURSE APPEARS
ON THE RIGHT.

manner, Fentress Bradburn designed an elongated structure that reaches out into the landscape and provides architectural and functional continuity among all facilities at the site. The building is supported by pilotis to allow uninterrupted traffic flow and landscaping beneath. The building's six levels function, in part, as corridors to connect parking structures, hotels, terminals and office space. Areas for ticketing, check-in, baggage claim, rental-car facilities and 2,314,000 square feet of office space are also included in the design.

The simplicity of the design promotes clarity of function. The architects paid particular attention to establishing clearly denoted circulation paths. Once travelers have entered the building, they are drawn down a single path along the building edge. Amenities such as satellite check-in, car-rental facilities and retail shopping are all located along this linear path to help travelers navigate quickly and effortlessly. A glass curtain wall exterior brings light deep into the building and allows travelers and office workers to enjoy the landscape from inside. On the upper level, office corridors are separated by an open-air space that gives employees an outdoor retreat.

LEFT:
THE LINEAR TERMINAL, WHICH LEADS AWAY FROM THE EXISTING CONCOURSE, ESTABLISHES CLEAR CICULATION PATHS. ONCE TRAVELERS HAVE ENTERED THE BUILDING, THEY ARE DRAWN DOWN A SINGLE PATH ALONG THE BUILDING'S EDGE.

BELOW:
THE NEW CONCOURSE INCORPORATES 24 GATES.

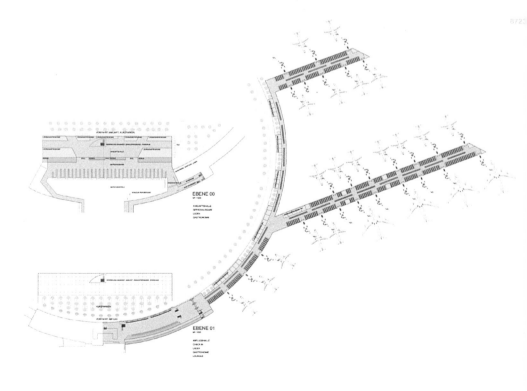

MUSEUMS + THEATERS

*"Designed well, a cultural facility reinforces
and enhances the experience of gathering
together for reasons that are other than
purely functional. A building's aesthetics,
the emotional response it evokes, should
work on behalf of this need to connect."*
- Curt Fentress

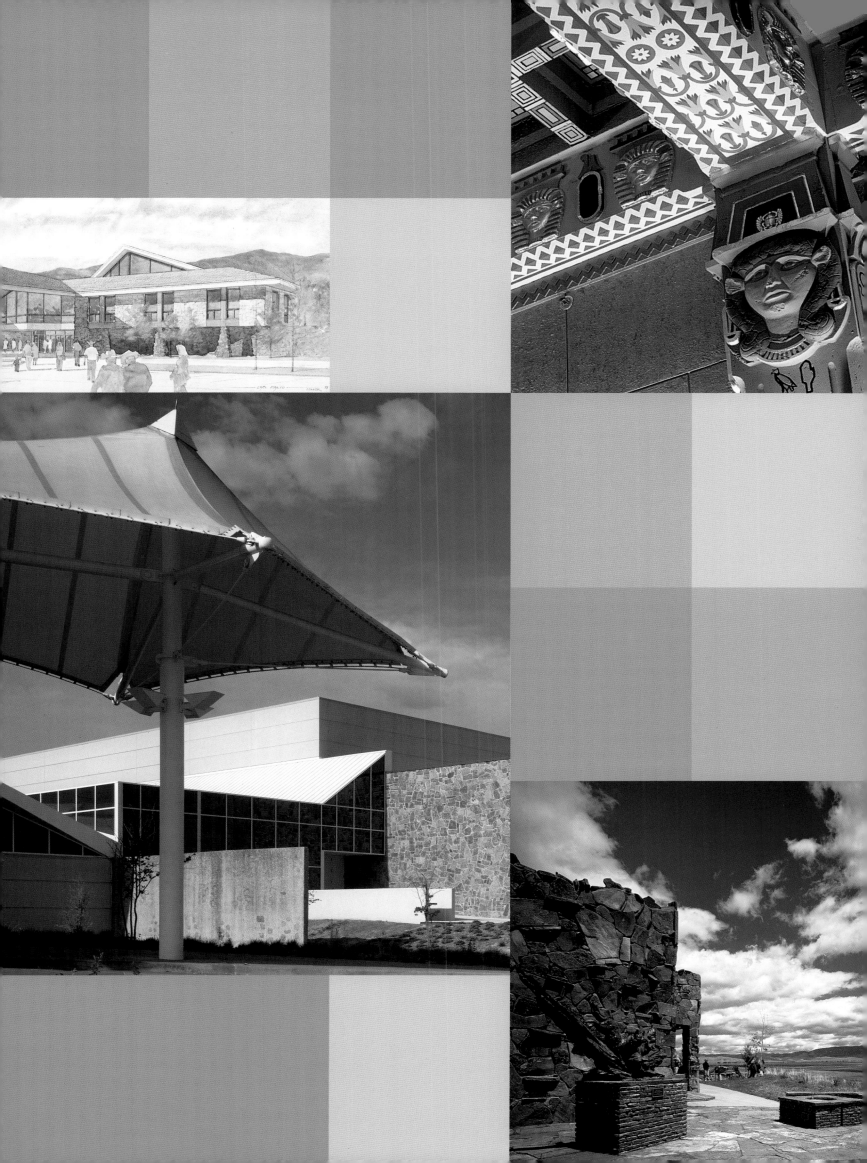

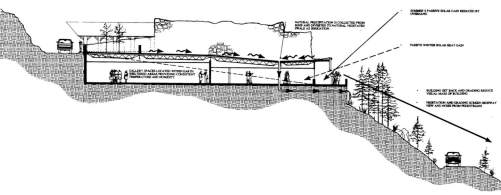

TOP:
THIS SECTIONAL
DRAWING OF THE
BUILDING ILLUSTRATES
THE DRAINAGE
SYSTEM AND SEASONAL
SOLAR PENETRATION.

ABOVE:
ON FIRST APPROACH,
THE BUILDING
APPEARS AS A
NATURAL OUTCROPPING
OF ROCK.

RIGHT:
SEVERAL BRONZE
WILDLIFE SCULPTURES
ARE LOCATED OUTSIDE
THE MUSEUM.

NATIONAL MUSEUM OF WILDLIFE ART

JACKSON, WYOMING

On a dramatic cliff overlooking the National Elk Refuge, the National Museum of Wildlife Art emerges from the earth like a natural outcropping of rock. The museum's location, coupled with the collection of artwork that pays tribute to wildlife, provides a rare opportunity to view wildlife in its natural habitat. Constructed out of rough stone, the building blends seamlessly into the native terrain, capturing the natural beauty of Jackson, Wyoming. The end result is an original, contextually relevant and timeless design.

In an effort to create a unique museum, the Fentress Bradburn team was sensitive to place and purpose. The practical, functional and aesthetic design highlights the Grand Tetons site and the art collections offered inside. The unobtrusive structure captures the subtlety of the landscape and natural light and features canyon-like interior spaces that house the collections on display.

The museum's roofline slowly emerges over the rocky terrain, welcoming visitors as they approach. The structure

**LEFT and CENTER:
STONE CLADDING
ON THE BUILDING'S
EXTERIOR HELPS
IT BLEND INTO THE
ROCKY BLUFF.**

has a playful nature. It first appears to be a natural formation, before revealing itself as a building.

Fentress Bradburn realized energy savings by setting the western side of the building into the hillside. The design allows for careful heat and humidity control in the galleries and storage spaces by placing those areas along the buried western portion of the building. Thus, temperatures remain stabilized and food service, retail, conference and other private office areas enjoy windows and outdoor terraces for the observation of wildlife, outdoor dining and educational programs. By bringing the outdoors into the museum, the architects created an open natural environment appropriate to the collections on display.

The team carefully chose exterior and interior details that coincide with the museum collection. An open-entrance lobby features animal tracks etched into the floor and a bronze mountain lion peering over a stone stairwell wall. The window-lined lobby allows natural light to flood the space. Its position also works to divide the space of the galleries and maintain temperature and humidity control in that area.

The architectural design of the museum had to address many important issues including concerns about the impact of developing a pristine wilderness area, the desire to create a building that embraces the spirit of the Grand Tetons region and the challenge of placing a structure within its site. Fentress Bradburn has crafted an extension of nature by designing a state-of-the-art museum facility with a unique awareness of environmental and ecological concerns.

THIS PAGE
ABOVE RIGHT:
THE ENTRYWAY WAS CONSTRUCTED FROM PINE TREES THAT WERE SALVAGED FROM THE YELLOWSTONE FIRE OF 1988.

CENTER RIGHT:
OUTDOOR TERRACES ARE PROVIDED FOR THE OBSERVATION OF WILDLIFE.

BELOW:
SOUTH FAÇADE. THIS SECTIONAL DRAWING ILLUSTRATES THAT THE GALLERIES WERE POSITIONED IN THE LOWER PORTION OF THE BUILDING AND ORIENTED TOWARD THE HILLSIDE TO MEET LIGHT AND HUMIDITY STANDARDS.

FACING PAGE:
A BRONZE DEER GREETS VISITORS AS THEY PASS UNDER THE MUSEUM'S WOOD-CANOPIED ENTRYWAY.

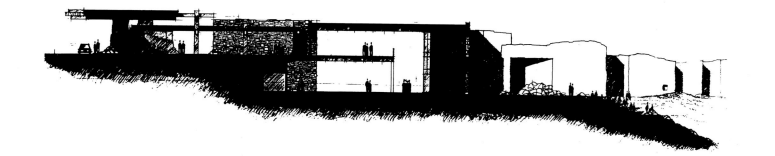

THE MUSEUM'S TOTEM
POLE IS HOUSED IN
THE TURRETED
PORTION OF THE
STRUCTURE.

ABOVE:
A BRONZE MOUNTAIN
LION OVERLOOKS THE
CANYON-LIKE LOBBY OF
THE MUSEUM.

BELOW LEFT:
STORAGE AND
CURATORIAL AREAS
ARE LOCATED
ON THE LOWER
FLOORS OF
THE BUILDING, AWAY
FROM LIGHT
AND WINDOWS.

BELOW RIGHT:
THE MUSEUM
FEATURES A SMALL
AUDITORIUM.

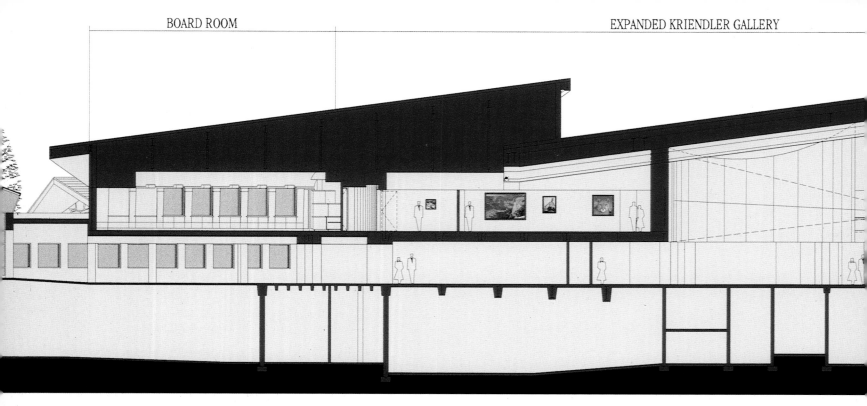

BUFFALO BILL HISTORICAL CENTER
CODY, WYOMING

The 237,000-square-foot Buffalo Bill Historical Center sits on a bluff overlooking the Shoshone River in northwestern Wyoming. Located 52 miles from Yellowstone National Park's East Gate, the museum is widely regarded as America's finest Western gallery, featuring the Harold McCracken Research Library and four internationally acclaimed collections: the Whitney Gallery of Western Art, the Buffalo Bill Museum, the Plains Indian Museum, and the Cody Firearms Museum. Fentress Bradburn's addition to the museum includes a new 50,000-square-foot Natural History Museum wing, an orientation theater and collection care facilities. The design also reorganizes the entry drive and parking facilities. The Fentress Bradburn team renovated and expanded the lobby to give it monumental scale, transforming it into a central orientation area for visitors, as well as communicating the uniqueness of the center and providing a site for special events.

The Natural History Museum addition engages new visitors with an account of Yellowstone's natural history, the Northern Plains, the Rocky Mountains and related basins. The design for the expanded Draper Natural History Museum mirrors the plan and massing of the Firearms Museum, but allows the Natural History wing to influence the architectural personality of the entire building. The central entry is thereby strengthened and an inviting front-door drop-off is created. New, three-dimensional, motion-hologram, interactive technology and special effects, including images projected on moving screens, will function as part of the Natural History wing's exhibits.

The ultimate purpose of the Draper Natural History Museum is to focus on humans' roles within the region — their impact on the land and vice versa. Fentress Bradburn created a new type of natural history museum that reflects a 21st century philosophy on nature and natural history. Flexible core spaces and temporary exhibit spaces interface seamlessly to create a flowing, easy-to-navigate floor plan. Demarcated by easy and understandable way-finding devices, the orientation lobby provides access to all museums, including the Draper Natural History Museum.

Named after William Frederick Cody, commonly known as Buffalo Bill, the museum captures his vibrant and multi-faceted life as a Colorado "59er," Pony Express rider, stagecoach driver, Civil War soldier, hotel manager, scout and actor. For design inspiration, Fentress Bradburn looked to statements Cody made in his later years. "All my interests are still in the West, the modern West," he said. Cody envisioned a new West, "with its waving grain fields, fenced flocks and splendid cities, drawing upon the mountains for the water to make it fertile and upon the

ABOVE:
FENTRESS BRADBURN'S ADDITION TO THE MUSEUM INCLUDES A 50,000-SQUARE FOOT NATURAL HISTORY WING, AN ORIENTATION THEATER AND COLLECTION CARE FACILITIES.

EDWARD L. GAYLORD
EXHIBITION WING

sweeping, peaked, curved canopy that is inviting to visitors. This architectural gesture reinforces a sense of entry that was not present within the original layout, while emphasizing the original reflecting pool and sculpture garden courtyard. The National Cowboy Hall of Fame's image is created in part by Leonard McMurray's magnificent Buffalo Bill Memorial. His work has been strategically placed to dramatize its scale and attract potential visitors traveling along the adjacent interstate highway. Inside, the firm's comprehensive design encompasses large, brightly-lit exhibition spaces and clearly defined passageways.

Many other works of art within the museum unify the structure and the surrounding environment. Evidence of this is clearly seen in "The Remuda" by artist Tom Ryan. The exhibition wing generated a 400-foot-by-26-foot wall. To integrate the character of the museum's architecture with the artwork, and to break up the monolithic quality of such a large façade, the architects separated the wall into five planes. Ryan's work now graces the five bays of the west wing and depicts 30 galloping horses and two cowhands, one leading and the other waving a lasso and following

ABOVE:
THE NEW ATRIUM, AT LEFT, BLENDS WITH THE EXISTING MUSEUM.

RIGHT:
THE LINES OF THE WINDOWS CREATE A GRID THAT PLAYS OFF THE TRIANGULAR ROOFLINE.

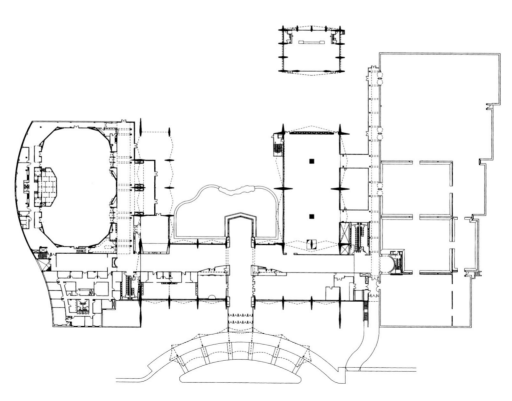

ABOVE:
THE CURVILINEAR
SHAPE OF THE
EXPANSION SERVES
TO SOFTEN THE LINES
OF THE BUILDING.

LEFT:
THE NEW ENTRYWAY
(CENTER) FACES
A NARROW ATRIUM
THAT HELPS ORIENT
VISITORS TO
THE MUSEUM.

RIGHT:
BRONZE STATUES OF HORSES AT FULL GALLOP STAND OUTSIDE THE BUILDING, FACING THE ATRIUM.

BELOW:
THE NEW ATRIUM CAN BE SEEN THROUGH THE WINDOWS OF THE EXISTING GALLERY.

ABOVE:
A POOL WITH
FOUNTAINS
SURROUNDS THE NEW
ATRIUM.

LEFT:
THE RENOVATION
AND EXPANSION
CENTERED ON
THE CREATION OF A
GRAND ATRIUM, WHICH
ORIENTS VISITORS.

and individual needs, such as catering. Each space is equipped with an individual sound system that provides independent acoustical control. This feature permits a multitude of activities to coexist without disturbing one another. The Executive Training Laboratory includes a multimedia training center, fully wired for the computer and audio-visual requirements of both large and small groups. A wall-sized pull-down screen allows this laboratory to accommodate almost any task or presentation.

When Peery's Egyptian Theater opened in 1924, it was considered a state-of-the-art movie palace, as much an event as the movie itself. With the growth of suburbs and the advent of the multiplex in the 1980s, Peery's eventually deteriorated. With the aid of Fentress Bradburn, the theater was renovated and reopened in July 1996. Restorative efforts aimed for a modern-day re-creation of the original Egyptian Theater, complete with the famous atmospheric ceiling, elegant side balconies and detailed proscenium arch. The exterior retains many original details, while elements of surprise and innovation were added. The original terra-cotta exterior has been refurbished, the papyrus-texture columns have been enhanced with vibrant hues and the six original Egyptian figurines still line the outside of the building. The performance stage, featuring a hydraulic orchestra pit and fly gallery, has been considerably

ABOVE LEFT:
EGYPTIAN DETAILING WAS RESTORED ON THE COLUMNS AND LINTEL, AS WELL AS ON THE CROWN MOLDING.

ABOVE RIGHT:
ART DECO DETAILINTG WAS RESTORED IN THE ORIGINAL THEATER BOX OFFICE AREA.

RIGHT:
HIEROGLYPHICS AND OTHER EGYPTIAN-INSPIRED IMAGERY ADORN BEAMS AND THE ORNATE COFFERED CEILING OF THE THEATER.

enlarged. The lobby has been expanded from its original form, complete with a replica of the 1924 box office. A new gallery area to the south allows audience members to mingle during intermissions.

To aesthetically blend the Eccles Conference Center with Peery's Egyptian Theater, elements of the theater's original design and construction were recalled in profile and form. The asymmetrical, curvilinear design of the two-toned, sand-colored walls, along with the cut-stone shape and texture of the theater's exterior, are subtly echoed in the conference center. Combinations of local sandstone, pre-cast concrete and curtain walls complete the structure. The strategically recessed bands of horizontal brick simulate Egyptian pyramid design elements, while blending the two buildings into one. On the interior, wrought-iron railings emulate Egyptian papyrus reeds, the elevator doors feature Art Deco detailing and strategically designed ceilings allow for indirect lighting to guide patrons between the theater and the conference center.

ABOVE LEFT:
THE STAIRWAY TO THE SECOND FLOOR OF THE CONFERENCE CENTER RECALLS THE ELEGANT THEATER DESIGN IN A MUTED FORM.

BELOW LEFT:
BLACK COLUMNS AND OTHER DETAILS SIGNAL THE CONFERENCE CENTER'S CONNECTION TO THE THEATER.

ABOVE:
THE CONFERENCE CENTER IS EQUIPPED WITH STATE-OF-THE-ART TRAINING FACILITIES.

RECENT WORK

*"Using a public building shouldn't be simply
a matter of having one's day in court,
catching an airplane, experiencing works of
art or watching a football game.
Great public architecture allows users to do
those things with ease. But it also
enriches the experience, heightening users'
awareness of the space in connection with
the landscape and the collective civic spirit."*
- Curt Fentress

DENVER BRONCOS STADIUM
DENVER, COLORADO

Fentress Bradburn was chosen to be the associate architect for the new open-air, natural grass National Football League stadium in Denver. The firm collaborated with HNTB Sports of Kansas City. With a price tag of $400 million, the stadium will hold 76,125 fans and reach the height of a fourteen-story building. Sports fans will feel as though they have entered a dynamic and futuristic civic space. The design team was also aware of community issues. The stadium is not merely a home for the Denver Broncos, but a modern facility that can meet the needs of the community at large by providing a venue for high school and collegiate sporting events, professional soccer, civic functions, concerts, trade shows and more.

The stadium's exterior can be perceived in three distinct ways. At 860 feet long, 780 feet wide and 165 feet tall, the structure will be a dominant landmark on Denver's skyline. Its distinctive, saddle-shaped top profile will compliment many other existing landmarks within Denver's "sports valley." To drivers traveling at freeway speeds on Interstate 25, the stadium will stand out as an architectural icon.

Fans approaching the stadium from parking lots on ground level are provided with a second view. Curved, open-air, pedestrian ramps have been integrated into the structure, giving the exterior skin a sinuous shape that reduces the perceived mass of the building. In addition, the natural anodized aluminum skin gives the exterior a silver sheen that reflects sunshine and produces a sparkle of light.

The third point of view is encountered as one walks along the base of the building. A 20-foot-tall brick wall creates a strong platform from which the building rises. The base features a two-color, soldier-course pattern that takes advantage of the Colorado sun and produces strong shadow lines. An aluminum trellised curtain wall sits above the brick base. The rounded bullnose posts and railings of the curtain wall produce a soft gradation of light that disguises the massing of the structure and creates a futuristic look.

The stadium's future-oriented design incorporates much of what has been learned about stadium architecture

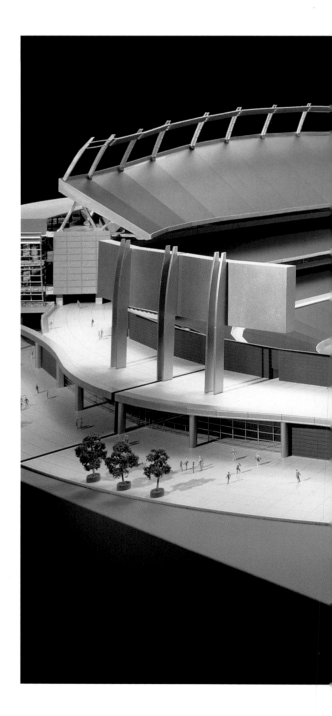

KUWAIT FINANCE HOUSE TOWER

KUWAIT CITY, KUWAIT

Inspired by the gentle swells of the Arabian Gulf waters, Fentress Bradburn created the design for a finance tower in Kuwait City, Kuwait. The 34,715-square-meter tower is 30 stories high and accommodates 20,490 square meters of office space and 14,225 square meters of commercial space. While life everywhere depends on water for survival, life in the Gulf is especially dependent on this resource. The tower reflects the image of water in its glassy façade and through its form.

Due to restrictions, the tallest building in Kuwait currently stands at 20 stories. However, the restriction was recently lifted to accommodate buildings as high as 30 stories. This allowed Fentress Bradburn to create the design for the tallest office tower in Kuwait, which reaches 155 meters. In establishing the design, the firm focused on representing the region in an unobtrusive manner. As a result, the center portion of the tower takes on a simple curved form and recalls the waves of the Gulf waters. Reflective metal panels and a glazed transparent curtain wall were chosen to symbolize water and tie the building to its surroundings. The cladding of the façade is elegantly detailed to provide a uniform curtain wall that reinforces the bold vertical gesture.

Beneath the bowed-out center portion are plainer forms clad in a vertically oriented combination of flamed and polished granites. This combination gives the base of the tower a sense of mass and solidity that extends upwards to represent the land that embraces the water.

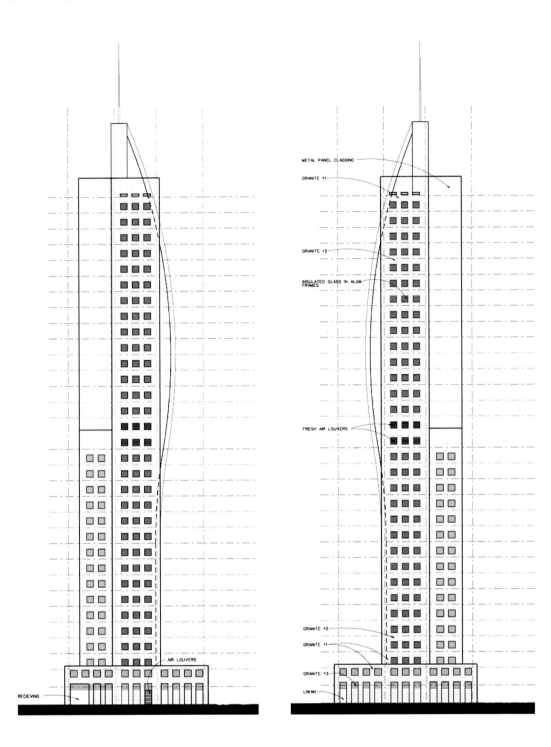

METAL PANEL CLADDING
GRANITE #1

GRANITE #2

INSULATED GLASS IN ALUM FRAMES

FRESH AIR LOUVERS

GRANITE #2
GRANITE #1

GRANITE #3

LIWAN

AIR LOUVERS

RECIEVING

ELEVATIONS
OF THE NORTHEAST
FAÇADE (LEFT) AND
SOUTHWEST FAÇADE
(RIGHT) ILLUSTRATE
THE 27 FLOORS
OF PRIVATE OFFICES,
GROUND-LEVEL
RETAIL SPACE AND
PARKING DECKS.

Located in the base portion of the tower is a commercial mall that accommodates over 14,000 square meters of retail space. Situated below the retail space is a structured parking deck that provides 81 spaces for tenants of the tower. Directly adjacent to the commercial mall is another below-grade parking deck and an adjoining surface parking deck that accommodate 216 cars. The remaining 27 floors are composed of private office spaces that total approximately 20,000 square meters. While the commercial mall stands out, because of its clean and polished flamed granite, the tower remains the most prominent form on the site, due to its juxtaposition to the base. The two elements of the 30-story tower complement each other and serve to unite separate commercial and executive functions.

THE CLADDING OF
THE FRONT AND BACK
FAÇADES IS ELEGANTLY
DETAILED TO
REINFORCE THE BOLD
VERTICAL GESTURE.

421 BROADWAY
DENVER, COLORADO

In 1992, Fentress Bradburn moved into a newly renovated building at 421 Broadway in Denver, Colorado. As the firm continued to expand its services and personnel, additional space was needed to maintain efficiency. In 1999, expansion and renovations began. Plans included a new main gallery space on the ground level, a new level of conference rooms, a refurbished design studio and expanded office space to accommodate 25 additional architects.

The entry level now offers an architectural gallery space, restrooms and a conference room, in conjunction with the pre-established reception and waiting areas. The gallery space displays the firm's work, as well as various traveling architectural exhibits. The firm also hosts regularly scheduled community viewings. One wall of the space looks out into the materials and mock-up courtyard, which is lined with displays of material samples, such as granite and marble. Furniture displays, maintained and arranged by the interiors team and selected furniture representatives, occupy the waiting areas. Pre-existing floor-to-ceiling windows are accented by a more open and inviting entryway.

After visitors have been greeted in the lobby, they are led up the main stairway into a studio work area surrounded by executive offices and five conference rooms. This new studio space features design models of projects in progress. Extending from the studio work area, a curving wall showcasing many of the firm's 142 awards for design excellence directs visitors into the architectural studio space.

The architectural studio and a materials and resource library are located west of the projects-in-progress gallery. New small workstations can be organized in project-designated clusters to aid in the collaboration process among in-house personnel. These elements line the central promenade, connecting to more than 70 architect and support staff stations. An additional 6,000 square feet will be added to the existing studio to accommodate 25 workstations for design architects. Skylights line the wall-and-ceiling junction to animate and enliven the space with natural undiffused light. Telecommunications for all stations are connected via a communication duct that runs beneath the floor.

THE EXPANSION ADDS VISUAL INTEREST TO THE EXISTING RECTILINEAR STRUCTURE.

The Fentress Bradburn team used clear open space and interconnected cubicles in their renovation of the marketing department, located directly above the 3,000-square-foot in-house model shop and half a level above the architectural studio. Vibrant primary colors mark the three main spaces' walls. The front entrance to the space is designed to serve the needs of employees, while acting as a gate that restricts access to confidential information. The space also includes a newly renovated conference room. Ample counter space throughout the area facilitates the assembly of proposals and public relations information.

A small room, located in a remote area directly above the studio and southwest of the marketing department, has also been renovated to house a newly assembled 3-dimensional animation department. Computer monitors line the wall adjacent to the entry door, displaying the department's current and recent projects.

As visitors exit through the centrally located elevator, the top floor of the expanded office offers them another small gallery space. This space also functions as a reception area for the 60-person dining/conference room and the outdoor rooftop deck that overlooks the mountains. A large pyramid-shaped skylight crowns the entire space. The dining/conference room incorporates the latest in telecommunication devices. Simple, clean, and well organized, the new top level provides a dramatic place in which to present design work.

Fentress Bradburn has transformed its building into a facility that is ready to handle the full-service architectural needs of the 21st century, with spaces designated for collaboration workshops, various displays and exhibits, model-making, marketing, three-dimensional animated graphics and work stations for a staff of 120 people.

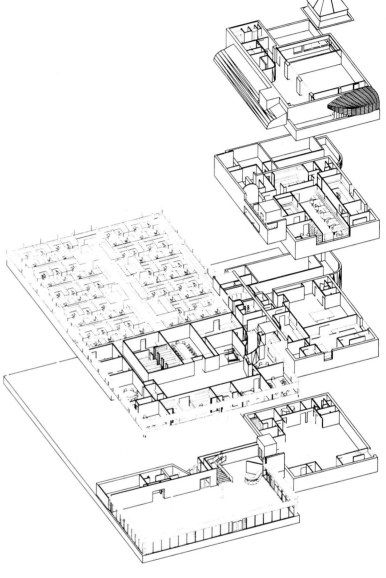

THIS PAGE
RIGHT:
PLANS SHOW THE
NEW GALLERY SPACE
AT THE ENTRY LEVEL,
THE EXPANDED STUDIO
ON THE SECOND LEVEL,
THE ACCOUNTING AND
MARKETING OFFICES
ON THIRD LEVEL AND
NEW CONFERENCE
ROOMS ON
THE TOP FLOOR.

BELOW LEFT:
SOUTHEAST FAÇADE

BELOW RIGHT:
421 BROADWAY
APPEARS AT THE
BOTTOM LEFT OF
THE PHOTO; THE
DENVER SKYLINE
APPEARS IN
THE DISTANCE.

FACING PAGE:
A LARGE PYRAMID-
SHAPED SKYLIGHT
CROWNS THE NEW
ADDITION TO
THE BUILDING.

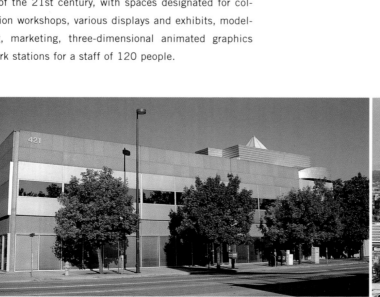

COLORADO CHRISTIAN UNIVERSITY

LAKEWOOD, COLORADO

Fentress Bradburn was recently given the opportunity to participate in a challenging design competition for Colorado Christian University's new campus. The design had to be sensitive to the environment, provide a good neighbor for the surrounding community and demonstrate stewardship of the land, a central facet of the university's philosophy. The completed design successfully met each of these challenges and fulfilled the aesthetic and functional standards adhered to in all of Fentress Bradburn's architectural designs.

Colorado Christian University had outgrown its previous site in Lakewood, Colorado, and was now relocating to 280 acres of undeveloped land, southwest of the Denver metro area. A small valley, between the Front Range foothills and a dramatic geological formation known as the Hog Back, offered the University a beautiful and complex new site. On the south edge, a string of ponds was connected to a seasonal creek, linking the campus to Belleview Avenue and an exclusive golf-course community. Lyons Ridge, composed of granite and sandstone and covered with scrub oak, pine and mountain mahogany, bordered the western edge of the site.

To the north, Turkey Creek and State Highway 285 provided the most likely entrance to the site. Along the eastern boundary, the Hog Back formation, a towering ridge of red sandstone, serves as the predominant landform. The Rocky Mountain foothills offered an environment unique to the Front Range of Colorado.

The master plan for a campus, which accommodates 3,000 students, dictated that the design encompass 800,000 square feet of building space and provide 750 parking spaces. Buildings in the area include a chapel, a library, an administration building, an alumni and visitor center, faculty offices, a graduate studies facility, a student center, a dining facility, residence halls and schools for theology, music, humanities, education and business. Space for a gymnasium, a natatorium, a tennis center, a soccer stadium, baseball fields and practice fields was also necessary.

Two distinct environments exist on the site, creating boundaries for design and construction. An upper meadow exists between Lyons Ridge and a plate of sandstone that is

A RENDERING OF THE ENTIRE VALLEY SHOWS THE CHAPEL, WHICH IS LOCATED NEAR THE ENTRANCE (LOWER LEFT), AND THE ATHLETIC FIELDS, WHICH ARE LOCATED AT THE FAR END OF THE CAMPUS (UPPER RIGHT). MASTER PLANNING FOR THE CAMPUS DESIGN WAS INSPIRED BY NATURALLY OCCURRING RAVINES AND WELLS THAT ALLOW DRAINAGE DOWN THE WEST FACE OF HOG BACK.

covered by mountain mahogany and tilted at a 30-degree angle. Running through the center of the upper meadow, from north to south, is a man-made ditch created over 100 years ago for irrigation purposes. Termed Bergen Ditch, it is now frequented by mule deer and other wildlife. The second distinct environment is a lower meadow between the Hog Back and the same tilted plate of sandstone. This area is isolated and possesses a natural sense of tranquility and solitude, as well as dramatic views to the north and west. A very distinct "notch" at the northern end of the tilted sandstone plate provides a view that extends all the way from the lower meadow, through the tilted plate, to the upper meadow and beyond. As visitors move south from the lower meadow, the view to the upper meadow is dramatically revealed.

Master planning for the campus design was inspired by naturally occurring ravines and wells that allow drainage down the west face of the Hog Back. Lush, vegetated environments flourish in this area. Fentress Bradburn represented the dramatic visual patterns along the face of the Hog Back with vertical lines in their design. The layout of the actual village, a series of planning grids

that shift in relation to one another, resulted from the topographic constraints of the valley floor. This shifting grid pattern produced locations that naturally stood out as central and prominent in relation to the overall campus.

The Fentress Bradburn team decided that the chapel should occupy a dominant position, near the primary entrance at Turkey Creek and State Highway 285. A second prominent location was designated for the library, which the architects deemed the second most symbolic icon for the Christian university. Surrounding each of these significant buildings is an area of open space. The Village Green occupies the space near the chapel, while the Village Square is featured in the open space near the library. A pedestrian spine, spanning the entire length of the campus, connects each of these "villages" and creates direct linkages that promote community interaction and a strong sense of place. The architects created a rich and diverse atmosphere throughout the campus with a variety of plazas, cloisters, courtyards and secluded garden areas. In addition, a series of arcades and colonnades unify the buildings and provide shelter for students, faculty and visitors as they tour the campus.

THE CHAPEL'S ARTICULATED WOOD AND GLASS FRAME RISES OUT OF ROUGH STONE, CREATING AN ETHEREAL PRESENCE.

The architects designed the campus' dramatic entrance so that visitors, as they approach from a frontage road adjacent to State Highway 285, get a brief glimpse of the Village Green just before entering into a wooded area. As the road continues to gain elevation, it exits the wooded area and curves sharply to the right, revealing the chapel, its bell tower and the village space below. Behind the village, in the distance, the distinctive notch of the tilted sandstone plate is revealed. In order to preserve the view of the village and the pedestrian feeling of the campus, vehicle access and parking was positioned along the perimeter of the village.

The chapel was designed to allow for flexibility and growth as the needs and size of the congregation increased. The initial nave portion included a balcony seating area for a congregation of 1,900 people. Expansion capabilities allow for the addition of two side wings that would bring the seating capacity to 2,800 people. In addition to increasing the number of seats, the side wings also provide maximum flexibility: They could be partitioned for use as independent lecture rooms or small auditorium spaces. The natural stone that exists in the area inspired the architects' choice of materials for the chapel. They begin with a very rough texture, which transitions into a more regularly patterned stone configuration. The design pattern symbolizes Colorado Christian University's philosophy of "being grounded on the

BUILDINGS CLUSTERED AROUND THE PEDESTRIAN SPINE GIVE IT A SENSE OF ENCLOSURE AND PRIVACY, IN CONTRAST TO THE LARGE OPEN SPACES NEAR THE CHAPEL AND LIBRARY.

earth, but with heavenly aspirations." The building's base represents the earth and the natural aspects of the buildings; the transparent crystalline upper portions represent the sky and the man-made aspects of the structure.

After entering the campus and taking in the dramatic chapel, visitors can access the administration, alumni and visitor center buildings located near the main entrance. The schools of theology, music and humanities were also placed in close proximity to the chapel, while the schools of education and business were located along the pedestrian spine to provide easy access to graduate studies, the student center, faculty offices and residence halls. The south end of the pedestrian spine features the gymnasium and natatorium center, which lead to the recreational practice fields.

Athletic facilities were positioned on the south end of the site to minimize the visual and physical impact on the natural environment and the neighboring community of Willow Springs. Placing the facilities there also created an opportunity to share recreational facilities with the community. To avoid excess automobile traffic within the village, special events parking was placed at Belleview Avenue on the south end of the campus.

ABOVE:
THE MOST PROMINENT
BUILDING ON THE
COLORADO CHRISTIAN
UNIVERSITY SITE, THE
CHAPEL IS POSITIONED
NEAR THE ENTRANCE
TO THE CAMPUS.

421 BROADWAY
Consultants:
MECHANICAL,
ELECTRICAL, PLUMBING
Swanson Rink

STRUCTURAL ENGINEERING
Martin/Martin

BUFFALO BILL HISTORICAL CENTER
Consultants:
ARCHITECTURAL SPECIFICATIONS
Carpenter Associates

AUDIOVISUAL and ACOUSTICAL
David L. Adams Associates

CIVIL ENGINEERING
and LANDSCAPE DESIGN
Fisher & Associates

COST ESTIMATOR
CTA Architects Engineers

EXHIBIT DESIGN
DMCD
West Office Exhibit Designs

MECHANICAL and
ELECTRICAL ENGINEERING
CTA Architects Engineers

SPECIALTY LIGHTING DESIGN
Hefferan Partnership, Inc.

STRUCTURAL ENGINEERING
Richard Weingardt Consultants, Inc.

VERTICAL TRANSPORTATION
Lerch Bates & Associates, Inc.

**CITY OF OAKLAND
ADMINISTRATION BUILDINGS**
Associate Architects:
Muller & Caulfield
Y. H. Lee Associates, Architects
Gerson/Overstreet
Consultants:
ACOUSTICAL, VIBRATIONS
and BROADCAST
Charles M. Satler Associates, Inc.
ARCHITECTURAL SPECIFICATIONS
Carpenter Associates

CIVIL ENGINEERING
Ackland International, Inc.

ELECTRICAL DESIGN-
BUILD ENGINEER
Rosendin Electric

ENERGY ANALYSIS
Gabel-Dodd

FIRE PROTECTION CONTRACTOR
Scott Company

HARDWARE
Architectural Hardware Sales
Company

INSURANCE
Dealy Renton & Associates

IRRIGATION
Brookwater

LANDSCAPE DESIGN
Freeman and Jewell

MECHANICAL DESIGN-BUILD
ENGINEER and HVAC
Critchfield Mechanical - CMI

PARKING
International Parking Design

PLUMBING and
FIRE PROTECTION ENGINEERING
SJ Engineers

PRINTING
East Bay Blueprint & Supply Co.

SIGNAGE
Monigle Associates, Inc.

SOILS
Woodward Clyde

STRUCTURAL ENGINEERING
F.E. Jordan Associates, P.C.
KPa

SURVEY
Geotopo, Inc.

VIBRATIONS
Charles M. Satler Associates, Inc.

CIVIC CENTER PARKING STRUCTURE
Consultants:
ARCHITECTURAL SPECIFICATIONS
Carpenter Associates

CIVIL ENGINEERING
Nolte Associates

CONTRACTOR DESIGN-BUILD
Hensel Phelps Construction Co.

ELECTRICAL DESIGN-BUILD
Merit Electrical

FIRE PROTECTION
Parsons Nolte

LANDSCAPE ARCHITECT
Vignette Studios

MECHANICAL DESIGN-BUILD
Trautman & Shreve

MECHANICAL ENGINEERING
McFall Konkel & Kimball

PARKING CONSULTANT
Walker Parking

PARKING EQUIPMENT
Mountain Parking Equipment

PRECAST
Stresscon Corporation

**CLARK COUNTY
GOVERNMENT CENTER**
Associate Architect:
Domingo Cambeiro Corporation
Consultants:
ACOUSTICAL and AUDIOVISUAL
Shen Milsom & Wilke, Inc.

CIVIL ENGINEER
Martin/Martin

COMMUNICATIONS
Comsul Ltd.

COST ESTIMATOR
Arizona Construction Estimates

DESIGN COMPETITION
CONSULTANTS
Stastny & Burke Architecture
Steinmann, Grayson, Smylie (SGS)

LANDSCAPE DESIGN
Civitas, Inc.
Peter Walker and Partners
Landscape Architecture, Inc.

MECHANICAL and
ELECTRICAL ENGINEER
Garland Cox & Associates
JBA Engineering
Riegel Associates, Inc.

STRUCTURAL ENGINEER
Martin & Peltyn

VERTICAL TRANSPORTATION
Lerch Bates & Associates, Inc.

COLORADO CHRISTIAN UNIVERSITY
Consultants:
LANDSCAPE ARCHITECT
Civitas, Inc.

**DAVID E. SKAGGS
FEDERAL BUILDING**
Consultants:
ACOUSTICAL, VIBRATION
David L. Adams & Associates

CIVIL ENGINEERING
Martin/Martin

ELECTRICAL CONTRACTOR
Ludvik Electric

ESTIMATING
Jerry Pope

GEOTECH ENGINEERING
Aguirre Engineers

LABORATORIES
Research Facilities Design

MECHANICAL, ELECTRICAL
and PLUMBING ENGINEERING
Garland D. Cox
Riegel Doyle Associates

STRUCTURAL ENGINEERING
Martin/Martin

VERTICAL TRANSPORTATION
Lerch Bates North America, Inc.

DENVER BRONCOS STADIUM
Architect of Record:
HNTB Sports

Associate Architects:
Fentress Bradburn Architects Ltd.
Bertram A. Bruton & Associates

Consultants:
CIVIL ENGINEERING
and TRAFFIC ANALYSIS
HNTB Sports
J.F. Sato and Associates

CODE and LIFE-SAFETY
ENGINEERING
FP&C Code Consultants

COST ESTIMATOR
and SCHEDULING
Western Industrial Contractors

FOOD SERVICE CONSULTANT
William Caruso and Associates, Inc.

GEOTECHNICAL ENGINEERING/
HAZARDOUS MATERIALS
Kumar and Associates, Inc.

INTERIOR DESIGN
Compositions/Barbara K. Fentress

SECURITY SYSTEMS DESIGN
Lockwood Greene Technologies, Inc.

SIGNAGE and GRAPHIC DESIGN
Monigle Associates, Inc.

STRUCTURAL ENGINEERING
Walter P. Moore & Associates
The Sheflin Group

SURVEYING
The Lund Partnership, Inc.

TECHNICAL, ELECTRICAL, PLUMBING,
FIRE PROTECTION ENGINEERING
and LIGHTING DESIGN
M-E Engineers, Inc.

TURF and IRRIGATION SYSTEM
Millennium

TV BROADCAST and ACOUSTICAL
Pelton Marsh Kinsella

URBAN PLANNING and
LANDSCAPE DESIGN
Civitas, Inc.

VERTICAL TRANSPORTATION
Lerch Bates North America, Inc.

WIND ANALYSIS
CPP Wind Engineering Consultants

**DENVER INTERNATIONAL AIRPORT
PASSENGER TERMINAL COMPLEX**
Associate Architect:
Pouw & Associates, Inc.
Consultants:
ACOUSTICAL
Shen Milsom & Wilke, Inc.
David L. Adams Associates

BAGGAGE BIDS, MUFIDS
and SIGNAGE SYSTEMS
TRA

CIVIL ENGINEERING
Martin/Martin
HDR

CODES and LIFE SAFETY
Rolf Jensen & Associates, Inc.

COST ESTIMATOR
and SCHEDULING
Western Industrial Contractors, Inc.

CURTAIN WALL
Heitmann & Associates, Inc.

DAYLIGHTING and ENERGY
Architectural Energy Corporation
LightForms

FOOD SERVICE CONSULTANT
Thomas Ricca Associates

GEOTECHNICAL ENGINEERING
CTL/Thompson, Inc.

GRAPHIC DESIGN
TKD Designs

LANDSCAPE ARCHITECT
Pouw & Associates, Inc.

LIGHTING DESIGN
H.M. Brandston & Partners, Inc.
LAM Partners, Inc.

MECHANICAL and
ELECTRICAL ENGINEERING
Abeyta Engineering Consultants, Inc.

Black & Veatch
Riegel Associates, Inc.
Roos Szynskie, Inc.

PARKING
Carl Walker Engineers

SECURITY
Aerospace Services
International, Inc.

STRUCTURAL ENGINEERING
S.A. Miro, Inc.
Severud Associates Consulting
Engineers, P.C.
Martin/Martin

VERTICAL TRANSPORTATION
Hesselberg Keesee & Associates, Inc.

WIND- and SNOW-LOADS
Rowan Williams Davies & Irwin, Inc.
(RWDI)

DOHA INTERNATIONAL AIRPORT
Consultants:
AIRCRAFT SYSTEMS,
COMMUNICATION and BAGGAGE
Swanson Rink

AIRPORT PLANNING
Landrum & Brown

ARCHITECTURAL SPECIFICATIONS
Carpenter Associates

CIVIL, STRUCTURAL, MECHANICAL
and ELECTRICAL ENGINEERING
Dar Al-Handasah

CONCESSIONS PLANNING
Sypher Mueller

CONTROL TOWER
and FUELING SYSTEMS
Aarotec, Inc.

MECHANICAL PEER REVIEW
Riegel Doyle Associates, Inc.

QUANTITY SURVEYOR
Westbury & North Crofts

SIGNAGE and GRAPHIC DESIGN
Monigle Associates, Inc.

STRUCTURAL PEER REVIEW
Martin/Martin

**JEFFERSON COUNTY COURTS
and ADMINISTRATION BUILDING**
Consultants:
ACOUSTICAL, AUDIOVISUAL
Shen Milsom and Wilke, Inc.

CIVIL ENGINEER
BRW, Inc.

COST ESTIMATORS
Jerry Pope
M-E Engineers, Inc.

COURT FACILITIES
Space Management
Consultants, Inc.

ELECTRICAL ENGINEER
SUBCONTRACTOR
Ludvik Electric Company

FOOD SERVICE CONSULTANT
Thomas Ricca Associates

HARDWARE CONSULTANT
Architectural Hardware
Sales Company

LANDSCAPE DESIGN
Civitas, Inc.

LIGHTING DESIGN
Howard Brandston
Lighting Design Inc.

GRAPHIC DESIGN
TKD Designs

MECHANICAL and
ELECTRICAL ENGINEER
ABS Consultants, Inc.

MECHANICAL and
ELECTRICAL PEER REVIEW
Riegel Associates, Inc.

MECHANICAL SUBCONTRACTOR
Trautman & Shreve, Inc.

PARKING
Rich and Associates, Inc.

SECURITY
Schiff & Associates, Inc.

SECURITY SUBCONTRACTOR
JWP Electronic Systems, Inc.

STRUCTURAL ENGINEER
Richard Weingardt Consultants, Inc.

TESTING AGENCIES
CTC-Geotek
CTL/Thompson, Inc.

VERTICAL TRANSPORTATION
Lerch Bates Elevators, Inc.

KUWAIT FINANCE HOUSE TOWER

Associate Architect:
Pan Arab Consulting Engineers

Consultants:
STRUCTURAL, MECHANICAL,
ELECTRICAL DESIGN:
Pan Arab Consulting Engineers

LARIMER COUNTY JUSTICE CENTER

Consultants:
ARCHITECTURAL SPECIFICATIONS
Carpenter Associates

ARTIST
Andrew Dufford

AUDIOVISUAL
David L. Adams Associates, Inc.

AUDIOVISUAL SUBCONTRACTOR
Electronic Systems
International, Inc.

CIVIL ENGINEERING
Parsons Nolte

ELECTRICAL DESIGN-
BUILD ENGINEER
Consulting Engineers, Inc.

ELECTRICAL ENGINEERING
SUBCONTRACTOR
Merit Electric

GRAPHIC DESIGN
Monigle Associates, Inc.

HARDWARE
Architectural Hardware Sales Co.

LANDSCAPE DESIGN
EDAW, Inc.

LIGHTING DESIGN and ENERGY
LightForms

MECHANICAL DESIGN-
BUILD ENGINEERING
McFall Konkel & Kimball
Consulting Engineers, Inc.

MECHANICAL ENGINEERING
SUBCONTRACTOR
Trautman & Shreve, Inc.

PROGRAMMING
Steinmann Facility
Development Consultants

SECURITY and ELECTRONICS
Latta Technical Services, Inc.

STRUCTURAL ENGINEERING
Jirsa+Hedrick & Associates

TESTING AGENCY
Terracon

VERTICAL TRANSPORTATION
Lerch Bates & Associates, Inc.

NATIONAL COWBOY HALL OF FAME

Consultants:
ACOUSTICAL
David L. Adams Associates, Inc.

ARCHITECTURAL SPECIFICATIONS
Carpenter Associates

CIVIL ENGINEERING
JGVE, Inc.

CONCESSIONS
Tom Shores

COST ESTIMATOR
Jerry Pope

ELECTRICAL ENGINEERING
Garland D. Cox Associates

EXHIBIT DESIGNERS
1717 Design Group
Design Craftsmen, Inc.

FOOD SERVICE CONSULTANT
Thomas Ricca Associates

FOUNTAIN DESIGNERS
The Fountain People

GRAPHIC DESIGN
TKD Designs

HARDWARE
Johnson Hardware, Inc.

LANDSCAPE DESIGN
EDAW-HRV

MECHANICAL/ELECTRICAL
ENGINEERING
PSA Consulting Engineers

MECHANICAL
ENGINEERING DESIGN
Riegel Associates, Inc.

PAINTER
Wilson Hurley
Duane R. Chartier

SECURITY
Steven R. Keller & Associates

STRUCTURAL and
CIVIL ENGINEERING
Richard Weingardt Consultants, Inc.

STRUCTURAL ENGINEERING
for TENSILE STRUCTURE
Severud Associates Consulting

SURVEYOR
Topographic Mapping Company

VERTICAL TRANSPORTATION
Lerch Bates North America, Inc.

**NATIONAL MUSEUM
OF WILDLIFE ART**

Consultants:
ASSOCIATE LANDSCAPE
ARCHITECT
Richard Vangytenbeek

AUDIOVISUAL
David L. Adams Associates, Inc.

CIVIL ENGINEERING
Jorgensen Engineering

ELECTRICAL ENGINEERING
Consulting Engineers, Inc.

FOOD SERVICE CONSULTANT
Thomas Ricca Associates

GEOTECHNICAL ENGINEERING
Chen Northern, Inc.

GROUND-WATER HYDROLOGY
Hydrokinetics

LANDSCAPE ARCHITECT
Civitas, Inc.

MECHANICAL ENGINEERING
M-E Engineers, Inc.

SECURITY
Electronic Design Associates

STRUCTURAL ENGINEERING
Jirsa+Hedrick & Associates

WILDLIFE ASSESSMENT
Biota Research & Consulting, Inc.

**PEERY'S EGYPTIAN THEATER
and THE DAVID ECCLES
CONFERENCE CENTER**

Associate Architect:
Sanders Herman Architects

Consultants:
ACOUSTICAL
David L. Adams Associates

ARCHITECTURAL SPECIFICATIONS
Carpenter Associates

CIVIL ENGINEERING
Jones & Associates

CONFERENCE CENTER CONSULTANT
Tom Pickering

ELECTRICAL ENGINEERING
Becherer Nielson Associates

FOOD SERVICE CONSULTANT
Thomas Ricca Associates

GRAPHIC DESIGN
TKD Designs

MECHANICAL ENGINEERING
Colvin Engineering

LANDSCAPE and URBAN DESIGN
Civitas, Inc.
BMA

STRUCTURAL ENGINEERING
ARW Engineers

THEATER DESIGN
Theater Projects

THEATER RESTORATION
Conrad Schmitt Studios

**REGIONAL TRANSPORTATION
COMMISSION and REGIONAL FLOOD
CONTROL DISTRICT HEADQUARTERS**

Associate Architect:
Robert A. Fielden, Inc.

Consultants:
COST ESTIMATOR
Perini Building Company

ELECTRICAL ENGINEER
T.J. Krob

LANDSCAPE ARCHITECT
Civitas, Inc.

MECHANICAL ENGINEER
H.H. Irby

STRUCTURAL ENGINEER
Martin & Peltyn

**SEATTLE-TACOMA INTERNATIONAL
AIRPORT CENTRAL TERMINAL
EXPANSION**

Associate Architect:
Streeter & Associates Architects, AIA

Consultants:
ACOUSTICAL ENGINEERING
The Greenbusch Group

AIRPORT PLANNING,
BAGGAGE and SECURITY
URS/Greiner

ARCHITECTURAL SPECIFICATIONS
Carpenter Associates

CIVIL ENGINEERING
Rosewater Engineering, Inc.

CODE CONSULTANT
Bob Pielow Associates

CONCESSION and
FOOD SERVICE CONSULTANT
Leigh Fisher Associates

COST ESTIMATOR
and SCHEDULING
KJM Associates, Ltd.

ELECTRICAL ENGINEERING
Sparling

GEOTECHNICAL ENGINEERING
Civiltech Corporation

LANDSCAPE DESIGN
Don Shimono Associates

LIGHTING DESIGN
LAM Partners Inc.

MECHANICAL and PLUMBING
ENGINEERING
Wood/Harbinger, Inc.

SIGNAGE and GRAPHIC DESIGN
Andrew R. Goulding

STRUCTURAL ENGINEERING
Anderson Bjornstad Kane
Jacobs, Inc. (ABKJ)

**SEOUL INCHON INTERNATIONAL
AIRPORT PASSENGER TERMINAL**

Architect of Record:
Korean Architects Collaborative
International (KACI)

Design Architect:
Fentress Bradburn Architects Ltd.

Consultants:
ACOUSTICAL
Shen Milsom & Wilke, Inc.

BUILDING MAINTENANCE
Citadel Consulting Incorporated

CIVIL ENGINEERING
Sevan Engineer Inc. (SEI)

CODE and LIFE SAFETY
Rolf Jensen & Associates Inc.

CONCESSION
Sypher Mueller International Inc.
Crang and Boake Inc.

CURTAIN WALL
Heitmann & Associates, Inc.

ELECTRICAL ENGINEERING
Fine E&C Co. Ltd.

FINISH HARDWARE
Architectural Hardware Sales, Inc.

FIRE PROTECTION ENGINEERING
Korea Fire Protection
Engineering Co., Ltd.

LANDSCAPE CONSULTANT
Civitas, Inc.
Seo-Ahn Landscape Architects
Associates

LIGHTING DESIGN
LAM Partners

MECHANICAL, ELECTRICAL
and TELECOMMUNICATION
McClier Corporation
Swanson Rink

MECHANICAL ENGINEERING
Han-II Mechanical Engineering
Consultant Ltd.

STRUCTURAL ENGINEERING
Martin/Martin
Sen-Structural Engineers Co. Ltd.
Jeon and Associates

VERTICAL TRANSPORTATION
Lerch Bates & Associates, Inc.

WIND TUNNEL
Rowan Williams Davies & Irwin Inc.

**VIENNA INTERNATIONAL AIRPORT
TERMINAL COMPLEX EXPANSION**
DESIGN COMPETITION

Associate Architect:
Fentress Bradburn Moore

PHOTOGRAPHY and ILLUSTRATION CREDITS

PATRICK BARTA: 9

MILT BORCHERT: 56, 57

CARL DALIO: 59, 84, 85, 96,
106, 123,141

STAN DOCTOR: 9, 65

CURT FENTRESS: 8, 80

FENTRESS BRADBURN
ARCHITECTS: 11, 30, 35, 46, 48,
51, 57, 60, 74, 75, 78, 80, 88,
89, 92, 93, 95, 98, 100, 104-5,
106, 107, 111, 118, 123, 129,
130, 132, 133, 136, 138, 140

JEFF GOLDBERG/ESTO: 26, 27,
29, 30, 35, 37, 38, 39, 97, 98,
100, 102

KEN GRAY: 127

STEVE HALL/HEDRICH BLESSING:
97, 116, 117, 118, 119, 120, 121

LISA HILLMER: 10, 11, 17,
123, 128, 129, 136

TIMOTHY HURSLEY: 10, 11, 16,
17, 36, 37, 38, 39, 40, 41, 46,
50, 73, 75, 77, 78, 79, 100, 103,
112, 113, 114, 115

RON JOHNSON: 8, 9, 11, 18, 19,
22, 28, 29, 32, 33, 48, 49, 59,
61, 62, 63, 64, 66, 69, 71, 80,
81, 85, 86-87, 90-91, 92-93, 94
105, 125, 139

ELIZABETH GIL LUI: 110,
111, 113

TERRY LUMME: 125

NICK MERRICK/HEDRICH
BLESSING: 9, 10, 13, 14, 17, 20,
21, 23, 24, 25, 29, 31, 33, 37,
39, 40, 42, 43, 44, 45, 47, 48,
49, 50, 52, 53, 54, 55, 59, 62,
63, 64, 65, 67, 74, 75, 79, 81,
82, 83, 97, 98, 99, 101, 103,
109, 111, 115, 121, 135, 137

QATAR MINISTRY OF
MUNICIPAL AFFAIRS: 88